SONSHINE!

Let the message of Hebrews warm your life.

James Long

art by Wayne Hanna

VICTOR BOOKS

a division of SP Publications, Inc.
WHEATON, ILLINOIS 60187

Offices also in Fullerton, California • Whitby, Ontario, Canada • Amersham-on-the-Hill, Bucks, England

Bible quotations are from the *New International* Version (NIV), ©1978, The New York International Bible Society. Used by permission.

Library of Congress Catalog Card Number: 80-52765
ISBN: 0-88207-576-4

VICTOR BOOKS
A division of SP Publications, Inc.
P.O. Box 1825 • Wheaton, Ill. 60187

Dedication

Thank You, Lord,
for my son Schaun,
and for the joy of seeing him
living in Sonshine!

Contents

A word of thanks
. . . as always, to my supportive and loving
wife Harriet, with whom every
project becomes a shared ministry.

Living in Sonshine! is designed to help you look at the frustrations and disappointments that can keep you from being joyful, and then to help you regain the warmth of living in Sonshine. You can read it by yourself or with a group. A leader's guide, with visual aids (SonPower Multiuse Transparency Masters) and Rip-Offs (student activity booklets) are available from your local Christian bookstore or from the publisher.

It is not God's style to cut us loose to drift through
the expanse of space
                    alone
He did not merely stuff a solar battery
into a sophisticated timepiece called Life
only to leave it on a dusty shelf
                              to rust
Instead, having created by His Word,
He stayed out in the open to speak
                        at different times
                        in different ways.
And when we ignored His voice,
when we accused Him of cutting us loose to drift
and leaving us on a shelf to rust
                        God spoke again.
He stuffed everything of Himself into
One Final Blazing Word that would eloquently say
                all that needed to be said
God spoke in Sonshine
                  radiantly
                  forcefully
                  penetratingly.

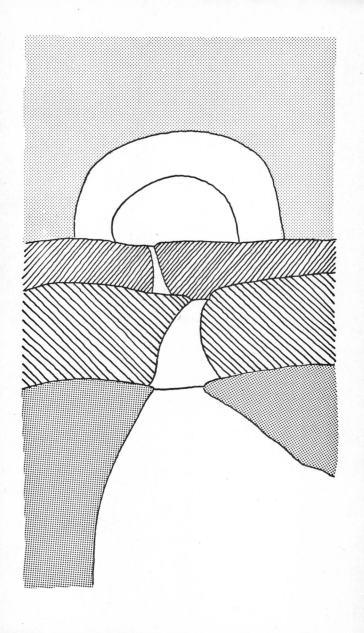

The late afternoon sun hung low on the horizon. The eastern sky was now deep blue. Yet, even that purple-blue sky was painted with faint wisps of pink clouds reflecting the setting sun.

Prodigal stood up, lifting his bulky pack onto his broad shoulders. He studied the plains that stretched out before him and the concrete thread of highway, extending for miles, linking the darkness in the east with the light in the west. He was ready to travel.

Then, not fully realizing all he was leaving behind, Prodigal turned east toward the darkness. Low over his right shoulder, the late afternoon sun still blazed red. Blood red.

1

Just when we needed to see exactly what God
Himself was like, He gave . . .

One Final
Blazing Word

Mark oozed excitement. And, as hard as it was to
catch him in a foul mood, I supposed he was genuine.

We sat in the tenor section of our small church
choir and occasionally missed a cue during rehears-
al because we were laughing about some crazy
comment. But that's just how Mark was. Though capable of being serious, he had more important
things to do than sit around feeling serious. Mark
enjoyed life.

I had linked his carefree lifestyle with his Christianity. But when tough times put the pinch on his
family relationships, Mark couldn't handle it; he
walked out on his wife and kids. Then he felt guilty
and soon left the church. He stalked off on his commitment to God's Son, not fully realizing all he was
leaving behind.

I suppose what saddens me most about Mark and
so many others who turn in their badges as followers of the Son is this:

God has already looked down deep into our frus-

trations and hurts. He has already spoken an encouraging, healing word.

"In the past God spoke to our forefathers
through the prophets at many times and in various
ways, but in these last days He has spoken to us by
His Son" (Hebrews 1:1-2).

The Book of Hebrews gives a detailed look at
this Word—God's Son—though it's not clear who
wrote Hebrews. You can look at the opening verses
of Romans, Corinthians, Galatians, or Timothy and
identify immediately whom the letter is from—in
those instances, the Apostle Paul—and whom it is
to. But with Hebrews theologians arm-wrestle one
another to try to decide on the author. He didn't
identify himself. Was it Paul? Or was it Barnabas,
Clement of Alexandria, Luke, Apollos, or Priscilla,
perhaps? Or was it Aquila, Philip, or Mark? It's just
not clear.

But we do have some insight into the people who
received the letter. And in it we read encouraging
and healing words God has spoken. In His people's
problems and powerlessness, God gave that One
Final Blazing Word. Some of them were considering turning away from Him, not fully understanding
all they were leaving behind.

Life was rough for these early followers of the
Son. Because they were Christians, the Roman es-
tablishment wasn't too fond of them. So, often they
were persecuted. Since they were *Jewish* Christians, they also met opposition from the non-Christian Jews who thought the Christian Jews had cut
off their noble roots.

To some of these hassled Hebrew Christians, the
solution seemed simple: Pull the shade on all this
Sonshine. We can almost hear their reasoning. "I
can get the Romans *and* the Jews off my back if I

just dump Jesus. No Christianity, no conflict."

Then this letter came:

"Remember those earlier days after you had received the Light, when you stood your ground in a great contest in the face of suffering. Sometimes you were publicly exposed to insult and persecution; at other times you stood side by side with those who were so treated. You sympathized with those in prison and joyfully accepted the confiscation of your property, because you knew that you yourselves had better and lasting possessions. So do not throw away your confidence; it will be richly rewarded" (Hebrews 10:32-35).

That was an encouraging and healing word to frustrated Hebrew Christians, as it can be to us.

Greater Prophet Margin

To these Hebrew Christians, part of the letter had a familiar ring. They knew about prophets, angels, priests, and sacrifices. But they didn't realize that the Son shines more brilliantly, that He is greater than all of these.

God sometimes gave encouragement and healing in the words of the prophets. My friend Mark would have found encouragement in dealing with his family problems if he'd obeyed God's commands through Moses.

"Love the Lord your God with all your heart and with all your soul and with all your strength. These commandments that I give you today are to be on your hearts. Impress them on your children. Talk about them when you sit at home and when you walk along the road, when you lie down, and when you get up" (Deuteronomy 6:5-7).

But the words God spoke through the prophets were incomplete. They came in law, prophecy, history, and psalms. They came in the writing of God, dreams, and visions. But there was more coming— One Final Blazing Word, God's Son.

What Do You Say After You've Said It All?

Ron slammed his fist on the kitchen table. "OK, show me where it says Jesus is God!"

I hedged. There were some visible inconsistencies in my life. Ron and I both knew that. And I didn't know the Bible as well as I should have, or as well as I liked people to think I did.

So chalk one up for Ron.

Several years later, Ron became a Christian. After Ron told me about it, he had something else to say. He admitted that all those years when he wasn't a Christian, and we had been friends, he hadn't felt that I fully accepted him.

Chalk another one up for Ron.

I'd missed a basic part of living in Sonshine: a burning love for those who've never walked in the Sonshine.

That brand of love—God's love—is clearly seen in the Sonshine. In the Son's life, we see love and forgiveness side by side and in perfect balance with holiness and judgment.

What Makes Jesus So Unique?

Through junior high and well into high school, I wrestled with a terrible fear that my life was out of control. I didn't know how to handle family tensions and often found an outlet for my frustration in going for long walks or throwing rocks at telephone poles.

It's a pretty lonely feeling to walk a mile or two on a dark night, juggling hurt feelings, unable to toss them to a friend. Or trying to leave some hassle behind, but finding it waiting when I get back.

If I hadn't made such a small image of Jesus in my mind, I wouldn't have felt so lost. It didn't sink in that Jesus had said, "Come to Me, all you who are weary and burdened and I will give you rest" (Matthew 11:28).

What makes Jesus so unique? Why call Him God's One Final Blazing Word? In Jesus, God and man are brought together. And we stand face to face with God's greatest revelation—His Son.

"In these last days, He has spoken to us by His Son, whom He appointed Heir of all things, and through whom He made the universe" (Hebrews 1:2).

Jesus is unique because He is the Heir of all things. Every jagged problem we encounter, as well as every legitimate joy, can be put under Jesus' control. When He returns, all things in heaven and on earth *will* be brought together under Him (Ephesians 1:10).

An even more startling fact is this: The Son's followers, Christians, are going to share in all this as joint heirs with Him (Romans 8:17).

Another reason why Jesus is unique is that He, as God, made the universe. This creating business involves more than "rocks and trees and skies and seas." To quote Paul, "By Him all things were created: things in heaven and on earth, visible and invisible, whether thrones or powers or rulers or authorities; all things were created by Him and for Him" (Colossians 1:16).

But there's more.

You Don't Sit Down on an Unfinished Job

A regular, homegrown, Old Testament priest did his sacrificing jobs while *standing*. The writer to the Hebrews introduces a Priest with such authority that He could complete the job all other priests failed to finish. This Priest is *sitting*.

"The Son is the radiance of God's glory and the exact representation of His being, sustaining all things by His powerful Word. After He had provided purification for sins, He sat down at the right hand of the Majesty in heaven. So He became as much superior to the angels as the name He has inherited is superior to theirs" (Hebrews 1:3-4).

Jesus sat down at the right hand of Majesty. How could He do that? And what work did He complete?

The Son is the radiance of God's glory, God's One Final Blazing Word in Sonshine. God "lives in unapproachable light, whom no one has seen or can see" (1 Timothy 6:16). "The Light shines in the darkness, but the darkness has not understood it" (John 1:5).

So the Son is God's representative. A puzzled disciple said to Jesus, "Lord, show us the Father, and that will be enough for us" (John 14:8). And the answer is likewise puzzling: "Anyone who has seen Me has seen the Father" (14:9).

The Son controls all things by His powerful word. The movement in the cosmic expanse of His creation is all controlled by Him. Jesus gave a few hints of this mind-boggling power. He spoke and stilled a storm, healed sick people, and even raised some dead people.

The Son purifies us from sin through His death. But He suffered from torn flesh, rugged planks, Roman spikes, and a cross of moral filth strapped to His back.

The Son returned to His position in heaven. So now He challenges us, "To him who overcomes, I will give the right to sit with Me on My throne, just as I overcame and sat down with My Father on His throne" (Revelation 3:21).

The Son inherited a better name than those of angels (Hebrews 1:4). At the mention of angels, it's likely that the Hebrew Christians perked up their ears. They'd heard a lot about angels before, and inheriting a more excellent name than angels was really something.

Angels Can't Just "Wing It"

Around the church where I spent most of my teenage years, it was normal to be rowdy, or at least mildly wayward, throughout the last half of junior high and the first three years of high school. Then, with a lot of prayer from the old ladies (bless 'em), the church thought it might be able to pull some of those adolescent rebels out of their tailspins in time to enter early adulthood, dizzy but dedicated.

A well-known youth speaker zapped me with an alternative. As a teen he'd asked the Lord to make his life a positive example. He wanted people to be able to follow what he *did*, rather than just listen to him tell what they *should do*.

Most angels learned this lesson. True, one big honcho angel, Lucifer, led a rebellion and pulled out of heaven with a band of rowdies. The entire creation is still seeing something of its result.

But the angels who stayed true know their place. They are obedient servants of God, not rulers with Him. *They* worship the Son, rather than trying, in some weird way, to compete. We could learn a lot from them. The Book of Hebrews was written to help Christians see things in their proper perspective. Since Jesus is greater than the prophets and angels, if we have any smarts we'll see our need to obey that One Final Blazing Word.

The writer to the Hebrews spells it out this way:

God's Son Is Better than Angels

"So He became as much superior to the angels as the name He has inherited is superior to theirs" (1:4).

Verses 2-3 say it: Jesus has a better name than angels: "Son" (1:2).

Jesus, the Son, is also "heir" (1:2).

Verses 5-14 explain it: "For to which of the angels did God ever say, 'You are My Son; today I have become Your Father'? Or again, 'I will be His Father and He will be My Son'? (1:5)

"And again, when God brings His firstborn into the world, He says, 'Let all God's angels worship Him.' In speaking of the angels He says, 'He makes His angels winds, His servants flames of fire.' But about the Son He says, 'Your throne, O God, will last for ever and ever, and righteousness will be the scepter of Your kingdom. You have loved righteousness and hated wickedness; therefore God, Your God, has set You above Your companions by anointing You with the oil of joy' " (1:6-9).

Jesus, the Son, made the universe (1:2).

↑

"He also says, 'In the beginning O Lord, You laid the foundations of the earth, and the heavens are the work of Your hands. They will perish, but You remain; they will all wear out like a garment. You will roll them up like a robe; like a garment they will be changed. But You remain the same, and Your years will never end' " (1:10-12).

Jesus, the Son, completed His job and sat down with the Majesty in heaven (1:3).

↑

"To which of the angels did God ever say, 'Sit at My right hand until I make Your enemies a footstool for Your feet'? Are not all angels ministering spirits sent to serve those who will inherit salvation?" (1:13-14)

The Point Is Blunt, but Jabs Deep

I've lost touch with most who were in my high school youth group, but I realize that quite a few turned their backs on Christianity. I don't believe they fully realize all they've left behind. One of them married, only to be divorced a few months later. Another kept her marriage going, but only for a couple years. One attempted suicide. Several are wandering aimlessly with no solid purpose for their lives. Perhaps the church failed us, and we certainly failed one another. But when I think of those friends, the message of Hebrews haunts me:

"We must pay more careful attention, therefore, to what we have heard, so that we do not drift away. For if the message spoken by angels was binding, and every violation and disobedience received its just punishment, how shall we escape if we ignore such a great salvation? This salvation, which was first announced by the Lord, was confirmed to us by those who heard Him. God also testified to it by signs, wonders, and various miracles, and gifts of the Holy Spirit distributed according to His will" (Hebrews 2:1-4).

When God, through angels, delivered the Law on Mount Sinai (Galatians 3:19), the people were terrified. They "begged that no further word be spoken to them, because they could not bear what was commanded: 'If even an animal touches the mountain, it must be stoned.' The sight was so terrifying that Moses said, 'I am trembling with fear' " (Hebrews 12:19-21).

Today, God's One Final Blazing Word is tempered with grace, so we're tempted to take it less seriously. Some people even pull the shade on the Sonshine and ignore God's Word completely.

Prodigal walked mile after mile into the darkness. Then he noticed a strange thing. Though he'd been walking for hours, that blazing sun was still clinging to the horizon behind him. It was lower in the sky, but it should have already set.

Exhausted and perplexed, Prodigal pulled the pack from his shoulders and sat down on a guardrail that ran next to the highway. Then something even more curious happened. Out of the twilight, on that long, deserted stretch of highway, a quiet voice spoke to him.

Prodigal whirled around to look in the direction of the voice. Immediately, he felt uneasy. Though the Man was standing in the evening shadows, Prodigal could see that the Stranger looked like him, unmistakably, as if they were brothers.

2

It started in a remote garden paradise with our original parents. It spread through all creation, through all generations. Even our own character has been influenced by the . . .

Mutiny on the Son's Planet

Four of us—two sets of brothers—pile into a '57 Ford (we painted the competition stripes ourselves) and drive a couple miles to the foot of the Whittier Hills in Southern California. We stop at a roadside stand and buy flowers. Farther up the road we turn into Rose Hills Memorial Park and retrace the route of Jan's funeral procession one month earlier. We locate her grave and sit down on the hillside to think.

From this hill we can sometimes see much of the Los Angeles area, depending on the smog. On a fairly clear day, the mountains can be seen to the right. But today they're covered with haze.

A question hangs in the air. None of us can quite put it into words. But even if we could ask it, who could answer the question: Why did Jan die?

A month earlier we had picked up Jan's husband, Bill, at the L.A. airport. He looked haggard. He described the last week at the hospital, but one scene

29

he told us about stuck in our minds.

Jan had been staring at the acoustical tile on the ceiling of her hospital room in Spokane, Washington. "It looks like a map of the world," she told her husband, "and all the dots are people, and they need Jesus."

Jan's kidney disease left her in pain, dependent on a hospital dialysis machine. Bill watched as the disease left her body a lifeless shell.

She died in her early 20s, one month before her first wedding anniversary, peaceful but concerned.

"It looks like a map of the world. . . .

"All the dots are people. . . .

"And they all need Jesus."

I learned a lot from Bill and Jan. Most of it didn't sink in until long after that smoggy day on the Whittier hillside. I saw in that young couple an example of what it means to be a Christian, even when wrestling with hard questions, intense struggles, and pain.

When I say, "God has spoken in the Sonshine," or "Jesus is God's One Final Blazing Word," what does it mean to a husband who watches his wife die? Or to a high school sophomore when her parents divorce? Or to a college freshman, suddenly paralyzed after an accident? Or to a fat teenager who is tired of being laughed at?

If God has spoken, what has He said about pain, disappointment, confusion, fear?

God's first answer to the question of pain, disappointment, confusion, and fear is that *we live in an abnormal world. There's a mutiny on the Son's Planet.*

God intended man to have authority over creation (Genesis 1:27-31), but something drastic happened when Adam and Eve sinned (Genesis 3). Sin and death became part of all creation (Romans 5:12).

Jesus—God's Response to an Abnormal World

The entire creation was doomed to eternal death. But God sent One Final Blazing Word, Jesus.

Jesus is not just a man God sent to show the world how to be good. He's the Ruler of the world. When the dust finally settles on the cosmic conflict, and the mutiny is crushed, the Son will rise, then part of the unlikely human race will emerge to rule with Him.

"It is not to angels that He has subjected the world to come, about which we are speaking. But there is a place where someone has testified:
    'What is man that You are mindful of him,
    the son of man that You care for him?
    You made him a little lower than the angels;
    You crowned him with glory and honor and
    put everything under his feet.'
"In putting everything under him, God left nothing that is not subject to him. Yet at present we do not see everything subject to him" (Hebrews 2:5-8).

God's future purposes don't include placing the world under the command of angels—even though angels delivered God's Old Testament Law (Galatians 3:19), act as His servants (Hebrews 1:7), and have a future purpose to fulfill (Revelation 8—9). We'll see how important this is when we find out a little bit about:

The Judges of Angels

We look at nature and wonder: *What is man? Why should God care?* Or we juggle the big philosophical questions of pain, disappointment, confusion, fear, and make the questions more personal: *Who am I? Why should God care about me?*

David asked these questions (Psalm 8). The writer to the Hebrews quotes the same questions (2:6-8). We can conclude:

• Compared with nature, people seem unimportant.

• Understanding what God has done for people, we know humans are valuable to Him.

That's why the mutiny is so tragic.

But God does care. He has stepped in to look after us and to help us. Even though we are "lower" than the angels now, in the last days we who are Christians will even judge angels (1 Corinthians 6:1-3). We'll share governing authority with the Son (Revelation 20:6).

So the first answer to pain, disappointment, confusion, and fear is: *We live in an abnormal world. There is a mutiny on the Son's Planet.*

The second answer is: *This abnormal world will someday be changed.*

Reverse the Curse

Admitting that the world is a mess isn't an entirely satisfying answer to a person in pain. The fact that we do live in an abnormal world is enough in itself to cause pain. But the simple reason why some people are not bothered by world conditions or the cosmic questions of pain, disappointment, confusion, and fear is that they are naive and unenlightened. If they were more aware of the deep questions of life, they might live in fear.

Odd as it may seem, there's some comfort in

knowing God agrees that the world is abnormal. If God were to say, "Well, actually I rather like it like this: War, hunger, death, and pain give the planet an intriguing flair," then we'd all feel hopeless.

We really need to know if God is still in control. So He reassures us that He is.

"Yet at present we do not see everything subject to Him. But we see Jesus, who was made a little lower than the angels, now crowned with glory and honor because He suffered death, so that by the grace of God He might taste death for everyone" (Hebrews 2:8-9).

Jesus is God's guarantee that this abnormal world will change, that the mutiny will be crushed.

But more than that, we sense that somehow, backstage, God is directing things to turn the mutiny itself to good. We see this in a fascinating parallel (Hebrews 2:6-9):

Mankind	Jesus as Man
Made a little lower than the angels	Made a little lower than the angels for a while
Crowned with glory and honor	Crowned with glory and honor
Everything on earth subject to him	Everything subject to Him
	Tasted death for everyone

The point is: Everything God intends for us to be is linked to Jesus. A relationship has been established. We have been made a little lower than the angels, crowned with glory and honor, and everything is subject to those who are His.

Jesus was also made a little lower than the angels, also crowned with glory and honor, and we know that all things will be subject to Him (Ephesians 1:22; 1 Corinthians 15:24-28). But there is a striking difference: He tasted death for everyone.

Forever Family Forever Holy

Someone protests, "I wouldn't expect the Messiah, God's Son, to *die!* Is that a display of strength? Or is the mutiny out of control?"

The answer is startling.

"In bringing many sons [and daughters] to glory, it was fitting that God, for whom and through whom everything exists, should make the Author of their salvation perfect through suffering" (Hebrews 2:10).

Jesus' suffering wasn't a divine mistake.

Through the Son's suffering, His family of believers has grown.

Those who receive Jesus through faith step wide-eyed into a great, galactic mystery: *Sonshine is the perfect Man—now our Brother.*

"Both the One who makes men holy and those who are made holy are of the same family. So Jesus is not ashamed to call them brothers" (Hebrews 2:11).

Being Jesus' *brother* isn't just a figure of speech. The Son said to His Father, "I will declare Your name to My brothers; in the presence of the congregation I will sing Your praises" (Hebrews 2:12, from Psalm 22:22). "Here am I," He continued, "and the children God has given Me" (Hebrews 2:13, from Isaiah 8:18).

So when the mutiny is crushed, the questions of pain, disappointment, confusion, and fear will be overshadowed by the answer:

We used to live in an abnormal world. There was a mutiny on the Son's planet.

But everything has changed.

"For our light and momentary troubles are achieving for us an eternal glory that far outweighs them all. So we fix our eyes not on what is seen, but on what is unseen. For what is seen is temporary, but what is unseen is eternal" (2 Corinthians 4:17-18).

But the answer to our questions has a present dimension too.

The Son Understands

Jeff had been in trouble with the law, and because of intense family conflict, he'd been placed in a foster home. Then he attended a Christian camp for the first time. He stayed in my cabin, so I tried all week to befriend him. But I just couldn't seem to penetrate his shell. I'd speak to him but he'd stare off into the distance in cold indifference.

Saturday morning as we were loading the cars to return home, one of the other boys in our cabin took me aside to say, "Jeff needs you." I walked the quarter mile back to our cabin and stepped through the door to find Jeff, this hardened 17-year-old, lying crumpled on his bunk, crying. He lowered his defenses and accepted the Son, but he still couldn't dredge all his doubts and questions to the surface.

Even as I tried and failed to understand his anxiety, there was Jesus with perfect understanding. A supernatural Brother.

His Equal/Our Equal

We are *not* Christ's equals. He is perfect in His holiness. But Christ *is* our equal in one major way—He is perfectly human.

Jesus voluntarily took on humanity—something that wasn't natural to Him—in order to defuse Satan's power over death. This suggests a process:

- The Son took on humanity in order to die.
- He died in order to rise from the dead.
- He rose from the dead in order to destroy death.

Jesus took hold of the weapon Satan was swinging—death—and used it to conquer him.

Jesus "shared in their humanity so that by His death He might destroy him who holds the power of death—that is, the devil—and free those who all their lives were held in slavery by their fear of death" (Hebrews 2:14-15).

This is reassuring, because actually there are two great mutinies. There is the mutiny of the Son's Planet which began in the garden with Adam, Eve, and the serpent. In this mutiny human forces, spiritual forces, and all creation rose up against God's original order and plan. The Son will crush that mutiny in violent judgment.

The other mutiny is our own personal coldness toward God. But He melts that coldness in the Sonshine of His love.

So we see a threefold answer to pain, disappointment, confusion, fear, and death—and even our own waywardness:

We live in an abnormal world. There is a mutiny on the Son's planet.

It will change.

The Son understands.

Hebrews 2: 14-18

After a long, uneasy pause, the Stranger spoke. "You are tired, Prodigal," he said. "You'll find rest in the Sonshine. But the farther you go into the darkness, the more exhausted you'll become — until finally you'll die."

Prodigal avoided the steady eyes of the Stranger. "The problem is," he said, "I'm not even sure I want to see Light."

The Stranger didn't answer, only took out a small, leather-bound Book and handed it to Prodigal.

"Who are You?" Prodigal asked.

"My name is Traveler," the Stranger said. Then, as He walked away, He added, "but there are some places I refuse to go."

When darkness finally came and Prodigal noticed he could no longer see the Light, he felt relieved.

3

The mutiny of unbelief has devastating
consequences. Only those who follow the
Son find rest . . .

Beyond the Wilderness of Death

Becki grew up in the church and was always highly
regarded. "Why aren't you more like Becki?"
church members would ask their daughters. And
clearly, she was an exceptional girl. She was not
only cute, which added to her All-American
"Christian" image, but she also seemed to have a
close relationship with Jesus.

Then there was Steve — gruff, coarse, uncul-
tured. Underneath his rough exterior, however,
was a soft kindness, a magnetic sense of humor, and
a rugged determination — all of which enchanted
Becki.

But Steve had yet another layer beneath the
rough exterior, and beneath his placid kindness.
This third layer hid a jagged temper which rose up
to tear at the fibers of his own personality and at
the emotions of those closest to him. Becki later

39

wished she had been exposed to this third layer before their relationship grew.

When Steve and Becki started going together, the church was shocked. The congregation's opinion of her dropped. No one was surprised when Becki became pregnant.

Alienated from their church friends by guilt and rejection, Steve and Becki were married in a small, quiet ceremony. Then they moved to New York to start over again.

There, in unfamiliar surroundings, married to a man she really didn't even know, Becki began to think. She remembered the hidden resentment she had felt trying to live up to the expectations of her parents and the church. She remembered how good it had felt to know Steve in such a deep, warm way. She remembered how she had stopped battling the question, *Is this right or wrong?* and gave in to what she wanted, recklessly, defiantly.

Now she was crying. She longed for a privilege she felt she would never again have — the privilege of living up to the expectations of her parents and the church. The restrictions she felt being a Christian placed upon her were minor, compared with the mental prison where she found herself rotting away.

One year later, divorced before the age of 19, Becki returned to her parents' home in Denver. She returned as a single parent with overwhelming responsibilities and paralyzing questions, suddenly feeling quite young.

God gives His Word, complete with its restrictions, for our *liberation*, not for our bondage. Bondage comes — eventually if not immediately — when we assert our wills over God's. The Son invites us to mix His Word with our faith, molding a new life from yesterday's shattered pieces. But how much better to give Him our life fresh, rather than recycling our guilt and sorrow after we've already messed up our lives.

A Place to Fix Our Thoughts

It's easy to blame the group, our families, or circumstances for our failures. Adam blamed Eve and implicated God. Eve blamed the snake — and probably kicked Adam. The snake, of course, couldn't have cared less. He'd accomplished his purpose.

The real temptation battlefield on which we're fighting is a battlefield of thoughts.

"Therefore, holy brothers, who share in the heavenly calling, fix your thoughts on Jesus, the Apostle and High Priest whom we confess. He was faithful to the One who appointed Him, just as Moses was faithful in all God's house" (Hebrews 3:1-2).

But why the mention of Moses?

The Jews thought highly of Moses. After all, it was of Moses that God said, "With him I speak face to face, clearly and not in riddles; he sees the form of the Lord" (Numbers 12:7).

If it was important for Israel to listen to Moses, God's servant, how much more important is it for us to listen to Jesus, God's Son? Isn't Jesus superior to Moses, as He is superior to angels?

"Jesus has been found worthy of greater honor than Moses, just as the builder of a house has greater honor than the house itself. For every house is built by someone, but God is the Builder of everything. Moses was faithful as a servant in all God's house, testifying to what would be said in the future. But Christ is faithful as a Son over God's house. And we are his House, if we hold on to our courage and the hope of which we boast" (Hebrews 3:3-6).

If we refuse Jesus, God's One Final Blazing Word, and don't stop our mutiny, we have nothing to look forward to but the wilderness of death.

Example: Israel

It happened at Massah and Meribah (words meaning "quarreling" and "temptation"). Moses stood before a gang of thirsty Jews and thought, *Looks like they want either water or blood!* Graciously, God instructed Moses to take his rod and whomp a rock. The people had water, but God wasn't pleased with the hardness of their hearts.

The scene at Kadesh was similar: Israel complained to Moses, "There are no grain or figs, grapevines or pomegranates — and no water to drink!" This time Moses was instructed to speak to the rock. Instead, in his anger he pounded it with his rod. He did get water. But he also got the word from the Lord that he'd never leave the wilderness (Numbers 20:1-13).

"So, as the Holy Spirit says: 'Today, if you hear His voice, do not harden your hearts as you did in the rebellion, during the time of testing in the desert, where your fathers tested and tried Me, and for 40 years saw what I did. That is why I was angry with that generation, and I said, "Their hearts are always going astray, and they have not known My ways." So I declared an oath in My anger: "They shall never enter My rest" ' " (Hebrews 3:7-11).

The Neglected Reality

We either choose to trust God or to ignore Him. One choice leads to life, the other to death. "I am the Way and the Truth and the Life," Jesus said. "No one comes to the Father except through Me" (John 14:6).

"See to it, brothers, that none of you has a sinful, unbelieving heart that turns away from the living God. But encourage one another daily, as long as it is called Today, so that none of you may be hardened by sin's deceitfulness. We have come to share in Christ if we hold firmly till the end the confidence we had at first. As has just been said: 'Today, if you hear [God's] voice, do not harden your hearts as you did in the rebellion' " (Hebrews 3:12-15).

There's a sense of urgency in these verses. Within nine verses (3:7-15), the word *Today* is repeated three times.

If we don't trust God right now — today — our distrust will breed more distrust. Our complaining will breed more complaining. Our hardness will breed more hardness.

This spring I noticed how long it took the snow that had been packed together to melt. Where snowplows had heaped it into small mountains, it took a long time for the sunshine to penetrate and melt it.

It's so easy to pack our thinking with the coldness of unbelief. The more we persist, the tighter we pack our arguments against faith and the more unlikely it becomes that a thaw will ever happen.

"Who were they who heard and rebelled? Were they not all those Moses led out of Egypt? And with whom was [God] angry for 40 years? Was it not with those who sinned, whose bodies fell in the desert? And to whom did God swear that they would never enter His rest if not to those who disobeyed? So we see that they were not able to enter, because of their unbelief" (Hebrews 3:16-19).

What about Rest?

Only those who have faith will enjoy the future rest that God has prepared.

"Therefore, since the promise of entering His rest still stands, let us be careful that none of you be found to have fallen short of it. For we also have had the Gospel preached to us, just as they did; but the message they heard was of no value to them, because those who heard did not combine it with faith" (Hebrews 4:1-2).

The writer is actually speaking of four kinds of rests.

Canaan was a rest (3:7-19). Unbelieving Jews didn't enter it. But Caleb, Joshua, and a new generation did.

The Sabbath is a rest (4:4). God worked six days during Creation and rested on the seventh.

Salvation is a rest (4:1-9). We stop working and rest in what Jesus' death and resurrection accomplished for us.

Heaven is a rest (4:10-11). It's the result of salvation. Man's great mutiny will be crushed. Then we'll rest in the light of the Son.

But rest doesn't mean inactivity. True, we don't work to obtain salvation, because we could never earn it with our futile efforts. But having entered the family of the Son, we do good works; they prove our faith is real (James 2:14-26).

"Continue to work out your salvation with fear and trembling, for it is God who works in you to will and to act according to His good purpose" (Philippians 2:12-13).

So why doesn't everyone trust God? The arguments for Christianity seem so convincing. But arguments alone don't make people believe. A person has to have faith in God. This is the only way to please Him (Hebrews 11:6). Some people have honest questions, others have nit-picking cop-outs. But still, behind them all is the faith problem.

"And even if our Gospel is veiled, it is veiled to those who are perishing. The god of this age has blinded the minds of unbelievers, so they cannot see the light of the Gospel of the glory of Christ, who is the Image of God" (2 Corinthians 4:3-4).

The Rest Remains

I remember listening with interest as an enthusiastic Christian attempted to lead a "self-sufficient" unbeliever to new life in the Son.

"Your life is empty and meaningless. Christ will take that emptiness away and give you rest."

"No," the non-Christian replied, "my life is really quite full and enjoyable."

The Christian, who had been taught that non-Christians were never happy and never had a sense of fulfillment, was flustered. But he countered, "There's a difference between happiness and joy. Inwardly you are searching." At this he quoted Augustine and Pascal.

The effort seemed certain to fail. Though the unbeliever was interested and politely listened, he was equally determined that the sad plight outlined by the eager Christian didn't apply to him.

There are people who don't believe in the Scriptures, yet seem to fare rather well. And some occasionally complain that "religious" people are more boring, less kind, and more gossipy than nonreligious people. And sometimes this is true.

Our faith in Jesus doesn't mean we'll breeze through life enfolded in heavenly wings of bliss, while unbelievers will always be tormented by guilt and a nagging feeling that there really is something missing in their lives.

Pluses of the Christian Life

Why is the life Jesus gives better?

Christianity offers a deeper dimension to life. Jesus makes life better. Given the same circumstances, Christians should be happier and more fulfilled than non-Christians.

It's OK to stress that Christ can change a life, but that is not the basic pitch. You can't wrap Jesus up and offer Him from medicine wagons or Christian bookstores as the cure for all spiritual pains.

Christianity doesn't depend on how life goes for us. We should follow Christ because He is Truth. The instant we assume the existence of heaven and hell — a timeless eternity — everything in life is seen in a different perspective. The question is not, "Do I have more fun — or a deeper sense of joy — than you? Let's stack 'em up. Tallest pile wins!" The question is: "What is truth? What does it demand of me?"

God has spoken the truth in His Sonshine — His One Final Blazing Word, who speaks today through God's written Word, the Bible.

"The Word of God is living and active. Sharper than any double-edged sword, it penetrates even to dividing soul and spirit, joints and marrow; it judges the thoughts and attitudes of the heart. Nothing in all Creation is hidden from God's sight. Everything is uncovered and laid bare before the eyes of Him to whom we must give account" (Hebrews 4:12-13).

Those who assert their will against God and yet prosper may never face up to their own mutiny until it's too late. Theirs is a quiet revolt. They're merely asleep in the Wilderness of Death — content.

In the darkness, Prodigal again thought of his unusual encounter with the Visitor named Traveler Then he remembered the Book Traveler had given him. Feeling around in his backpack, Prodigal pulled out a flashlight and opened the small leather-bound Book.

"There is help in conflict, rest in weariness, comfort in pain," he read. "Sonshine," the book continued, "is not far away."

Prodigal bristled at the mention of Sonshine. The Book had described precisely what he was running away from. He tossed the Book aside, flicked off the flashlight, and leaned against his pack to sleep. But he did not sleep well. He woke in the middle of the night, terrified by the darkness he had craved. It was as though he realized for the first time how dense darkness could be.

And how cold.

For what seemed like hours, Prodigal gazed into the blackness. Then, as he finally started to doze again, he noticed on the horizon a faint flicker of Light.

He slept fitfully.

4

We should never wonder, Does God care about
our hardships, our indifference toward Him, our
own twisted nature? His life proved . . .

The Son
Cries Too

Just outside a small northern Indiana town where I
lived for five years is a certain country road. It is a
straight asphalt strip across farmland that is slowly
being converted into homesites. But just before
that north-south road dead-ends into an east-west
highway, it takes a sudden dip and makes a slight
turn across a narrow bridge over a slow-moving
stream. On the other side of the bridge, the road
climbs sharply, curves again, and meets the east-
west highway. At the legal speed limit, the dips and
curves in the road are easily negotiated.

Ed and Linda, both raised in this northern Indiana community, met in high school and married
young, over the protests of their parents. Their relationship started out rough and got rougher. It was
like a junior high love affair: They were together
one week, followed by a fight and breakup the
next.

Then Cindy was born.

Linda hoped the marriage would stabilize, for the

51

sake of the baby. But it didn't. Two years later, Linda
was pregnant again and hoping their marriage would
hold together. But Ed and Linda continued to fight
until one Thursday evening Ed left, childishly taunt-
ing, "I don't ever want to see you again! I hate you!"

Later that night, Ed and three friends loaded a case
of beer in a battered car and left for a joyride on the
country roads. It was 4 A.M. when they tore along
that north-south road. As they neared the bridge
where the road turned, they lost control of the car. It
left the highway and careened airborne across the
stream, crashing in a tangled heap on the far stream
bank, killing the driver and all three passengers.

I will never forget Friday morning and the days
that followed — hearing Linda's hysterical crying,
looking into her deep sunken eyes and blank face. I
searched for adequate words for a pregnant widow
in her early 20s with a two-year-old daughter. I
thought of Linda and wondered:

Could she ever accept new life in the Son?

*Was her wound too raw, her anxiety too intense,
her understanding too limited?*

*Could she ever really trust a Potter who shat-
tered his pottery for some unknown purpose?*

But I knew Jesus could break her shell and soothe
the hurt with His quiet message of understanding
love. We don't have to defend Him with shallow reasoning. We can't. Only Jesus can make someone willing to wait for the ultimate answer to the one-word
question, "Why?"

But Jesus often whispers His message of understanding love through sensitive people. There's no
place for easy answers, such as "Just trust the Lord."

Instead, He tells us, "Rejoice with those who rejoice; mourn with those who mourn" (Romans
12:15). Then the writer to the Hebrews reminds us

of a startling reality: We are not the only ones who weep when others weep; the Son cries too.

Two Plus Two and Three More

When the hard times became intense, the Hebrew Christians began questioning, "Wasn't life simpler without Jesus? Shouldn't we cash in our Christianity? If Jesus is Lord, why all the hassles?"

Not only was the Book of Hebrews written to stress the uniqueness of Jesus, but also to remind those in conflict, weariness, and pain: *The Son cries too.*

The writer to the Hebrews makes this point with two encouragements, two explanations, and three unusual facts.

Encouragement #1: *Keep your commitment!* "Therefore, since we have a great High Priest who has gone through the heavens, Jesus the Son of God, let us hold firmly to the faith we profess" (Hebrews 4:14).

This gives us another reason to follow the Son. It stacks up like this:

The Son and Angels	The Son and Moses
The Son is greater than angels (1:5-14).	The Son is greater than Moses (3:1-6).
Warning: Pay attention to Him (2:1-5).	*Warning:* Believe and obey Him (3:7-19).
In the Son we too are raised above angels (2:6-16).	In the Son we are led into perfect rest (4:1-13).
The Son is our High Priest (2:17-18).	The Son is our High Priest (4:14-16).

Priests represented God to the people and the people to God. Jesus is the unique High Priest to end all high priests. Instead of walking into a stone temple (or canvas tent), then passing through a curtain from the Holy Place into the Holy of Holies, this great High Priest has gone into heaven. The Son stands up for us in heaven.

Able Not To/Not Able To

Explanation #1: *The Priest cares!* "For we do not have a High Priest who is unable to sympathize with our weaknesses, but we have One who has been tempted in every way, just as we are — yet was without sin" (Hebrews 4:15).

People have argued, "What about Jesus' temptation? To put it bluntly, if it wasn't possible for Jesus to sin, what's the big deal about His temptation?

The Tempter says, "Here's a hunk of granite, make it Jewish rye." Then the Tempter puts Him on a tall building and taunts, "Leap down, Superman-style, with a single bound. The angels will help." Then he puts Jesus on a high mountain and shows Him the world's kingdoms, saying, "Worship me and they're Yours!"

We might ask, "Were the kingdoms his to give? Could Jesus have made a safe touchdown from a high house? Can He make bread with some hocus-pocus over a fistful of stone?"

But that's not the point. Satan tempted Jesus to bypass the Cross, to act independently of the Father. Any little sin would do.

Think of that in relation to one significant night. Within hours Jesus was to die, nailed to a wooden cross. He would take the punishment for *our* mutiny. "My soul is overwhelmed with sorrow to the point of death," He told His followers (Matthew 26:38). "He fell with His face to the ground and prayed, 'My Father, if it is possible, may this cup be taken from Me. Yet not as I will, but as You will' " (26:39). Luke adds, "An angel from heaven appeared to Him and strengthened Him. And being in anguish, He prayed more earnestly, and His sweat was like drops of blood falling to the ground" (Luke 22:43-44).

Why such intense anguish? Was it the physical pain? Or was it the spiritual and emotional horror of His sinless character taking our sin? Or both? (2 Corinthians 5:21)

If Jesus had sinned, would we value His help when we are tempted? Because Jesus was tempted without sinning we are encouraged to keep our commitment.

Have Mercy

While in college in Southern California, I was active in street evangelism. I spent almost every Friday night with people in downtown Los Angeles. Saturday nights were spent in Hollywood. And there was a sharp contrast between the two locations. In L.A. we often spoke with down-and-outers, drunks, minorities, and the elderly who lived in the city.

The Hollywood crowd was younger and flamboyant, with more drug problems and a heavier concentration of cults — Children of God, Hare Krishna, and others. But there were striking similarities in the ways people reacted to Jesus.

In both places I found many who trusted Jesus and many who didn't. But it still stuns me to think of their reasons for turning Christianity down.

There were intellectual questions and moral hang-
ups. But behind these was a common thread of unfortunate past experiences with religion — a mood
of apprehension and caution: "Assuming He's out
there somewhere, can I really trust Jesus?"

In contrast to these misconceptions is . . .

Encouragement #2: *Come closer!* Let us then
approach the throne of grace with confidence so
that we may receive mercy and find grace to help
us in our time of need" (Hebrews 4:16).

We shrink from punishment. But we run to mercy; we celebrate grace. God is not a cosmic execu-
tioner. He is the Father who cares. Through His
mercy we can escape the judgment we deserve.
Through His grace we can find help to do right and
to handle hardships.

So why do some people twist Christianity into a
joyless ordeal to be avoided? Why do some people
hide from His mercy and grace? Why the mood of
fear and caution?

After Jesus' triumphal entry into Jerusalem, He
sat on a hillside and wept over the city because of
the people's unbelief.

"If you, even you, had only known on this day
what would bring you peace — but now it is hidden
from your eyes. The days will come upon you when
your enemies will build an embankment against
you and encircle you and hem you in on every side.
They will dash you to the ground, you and the children within your walls. They will not leave one
stone on another, because you did not recognize
the time of God's coming to you" (Luke 19:42-44).

In A.D. 70 it happened as He predicted. Jerusalem was devastated.

Today God invites us to come closer, to find mercy and grace.

And Now a Word on Religious Leaders

Explanation #2: *The Priest helps!*
"Every high priest is selected from among men and is appointed to represent them in matters related to God, to offer gifts and sacrifices for sins. He is able to deal gently with those who are ignorant and are going astray, since he himself is subject to weakness. This is why he has to offer sacrifices for his own sins, as well as for the sins of the people. No one takes this honor upon himself; he must be called by God, just as Aaron was" (Hebrews 5:1-4).

Religious leaders are to be compassionate, caring, gentle people (2 Timothy 2:24-26). They should sympathize with others' weaknesses because they know their own. But religious leaders are often narrow, critical, intolerant. Some have forgotten their own weaknesses.

But something has happened to change the whole character of religion in the world. Jesus introduced something new, God's One Final Blazing Word, our great High Priest.

"So Christ also did not take upon Himself the glory of becoming a High Priest. But God said to Him, 'You are My Son; today I have become Your Father.' And He says in another place, 'You are a Priest forever, just like Melchizedek' " (Hebrews 5:5-6).

Three Unusual Facts

While involved in street evangelism, I had a long conversation with an 18-year-old named Joe. His drug habit was so strong, and Jesus seemed so far away from him that I became uneasy. I wondered if

I should have been talking to someone more responsive. Joe left with a promise to think about Jesus. I forgot about him.

I was shocked to learn months later that Joe's life had made a sudden, dramatic turnabout. He had thrown the pills away and had enrolled in a Bible college to prepare for the ministry.

The Son had torn at Joe's life with invincible tenderness. Jesus had pulled down Joe's defenses and melted his mood of fear and caution. The change was possible because of three unusual facts:

Unusual fact #1: *Jesus' prayers.* "During the days of Jesus' life on earth, He offered up prayers and petitions with loud cries and tears to the One who could save Him from death, and He was heard because of His reverent submission" (Hebrews 5:7).

Jesus cries for our hardships. He cries for our coldness, our indifference. He cries for our coming destruction, our judgment, if we don't know Him. But beyond all this, He cries for our sin, our moral dirt. But it is more than "moral dirt." It is an inward wrongness, a twisted nature. For that He died. But remember the night before the death — His prayer, His anguish, His sweat, His reverent submission.

Unusual fact #2: *Jesus' perfection.* Though He was a Son, He learned obedience from what He suffered and, once made perfect, He became the Source of eternal salvation for all who obey Him" (Hebrews 5:8-9).

"Once made perfect," has nothing to do with Jesus' morality, as if to say there was a time when He wasn't perfect. The point is this: Once He learned suffering by experience, He was *perfectly* qualified as a Priest. The result: He is the Source of eternal salvation to everyone who, through faith, will leave his mutiny behind and step out of the

Wilderness of Death and into new life in the Son.

Unusual fact #3: *Jesus' priesthood*. "And [He] was designated by God to be High Priest in the order of Melchizedek" (Hebrews 5:10).

But who was this Melchizedek? And what is the priesthood of Jesus? The writer to the Hebrews interrupts the explanation to deal with the problem of Christians who refuse to grow up in their new lives — those who dabble in their own personal mutinies and play on the doorstep of the Wilderness of Death.

Prodigal awoke with blazing Sonshine pounding down on his body. He tried to protect his eyes from the penetrating rays, but even with his eyes closed tightly and covered by his hands, his world still blazed red.

There was something piercing and even embarrassing about the Sonshine. It not only shattered the darkness, but it also exposed his most intimate motives and attitudes. Prodigal was facing more than lifeless rays from a distant fireball. He was facing a living Light.

Later, Prodigal realized that many things can only be seen in Sonshine. Surrounding Prodigal was a world of activity he'd never seen. He was aware only of himself and the intense Light that held him spellbound, demanding that he look at himself as only the Sonshine could expose him.

Finally, as certain as if some all-powerful Voice had spoken to him, Prodigal concluded: *I cannot leave this Light and live. But if I stay, I am sure that I must die.*

He stood silently in the Sonshine, and waited.

5

Our lives are planted seeds. Allowed to grow
naturally without God, we become thorns and
thistles. But when Sonshine penetrates that seed
New Life sprouts . . .

Out of the
Parched Earth

I sat at my desk, pulled out a yellow legal pad and
black marking pen, and began listing names. In less
than five minutes, I had listed 15 friends.

One was an accomplished rock guitarist.

Another had narrowly escaped death.

Several had been in trouble with the law.

One had attempted suicide.

Several were into drugs.

Others led ordinary, uneventful lives.

They were from Southern California, San Fran-
cisco, Indiana, Michigan, and Kansas.

Some were from church families, others from
non-Christian backgrounds.

But they all shared one common experience:
They'd changed their minds about Jesus. They'd
encountered God's One Final Blazing Word, thinking that He is Truth. But they had all turned their
backs on any commitment to Him.

63

Out of the parched earth of our rebellion against God comes either greater rebellion or new life. The choice is ours. But even if new life does sprout out of cracked soil, it may wither in difficult times, get trampled by old habits, or be choked by weeds of wrong values.

One of my friends, John, nearly lost his life in a family fight. The court placed him in a Christian foster home. Surrounded by loving friends, he seemed to become a Christian. But a few years later his commitment wavered. "Wrong friends," someone theorized.

Mary came to church regularly for a few years. But some people there questioned her morals. Sensing their judgmental gazes, she left. But in the process of coming and going, did she brush past Truth? Or did she accept it?

Jesus spoke of four kinds of soil on which seeds fall—the footpath, the rocky ground, the weed patch, and the fertile soil. Birds get the seeds that fall on the footpath. Heat kills the seeds that fall on rocky ground. Thorns choke the seeds that try to survive in the weed patch. But the seeds that hit good soil grow. (Read this parable in Matthew 13:1-23.)

The seed is the Word of God. The soil is the listener's attitude. Sometimes the devil carries the seed of the Word away from the place of need. Sometimes people make shallow commitments without counting the cost. Sometimes people choke the Word with their own twisted values. But sometimes the Word hits fertile ground and new life sprouts.

Yet, left to ourselves, all of us are like that parched, rocky soil. New life sprouts, pushing its way up from the soil that is both parched and fertile—parched from our rebellious mutiny, yet fertile in what God can do in spite of it.

But what happens when soil that sprouts new life stays parched and rocky?

A Peril and a Promise

The Book of Hebrews presents five strong warnings against walking away from Christianity. They are severe. Final.

Warning #1: Don't ignore Jesus (Hebrews 2:1-4).

Warning #2: Don't doubt God's Word (3:7—4:13).

Warning #3: Don't leave the Son (5:11—6:20).

Warning #4: Don't stay in sin (10:26-31).

Warning #5: Don't refuse God's grace (12:18-29).

Most of us can disregard God's warnings easily, for the sake of doing what we want to do. But there are consequences of disregarding the warnings.

If you ignore Jesus, your sins won't be forgiven.

If you doubt His Word, you'll not enter His rest.

If you keep on sinning, there's no sacrifice for those sins left.

If you refuse God's grace, you'll be judged.

The Bible warns us against rebellion and mutiny. True, returning prodigals are received and forgiven. But persistent prodigals are judged.

The third warning vividly describes the danger of running from the Son. It also gives an encouragement: Remember God's promise.

Warm Milk and Cookies.
Hold the Cookies.

Don't Leave the Son

The Book of Hebrews was originally written to Jewish Christians who were thinking about dumping their Christianity and sliding back into Old Testament Jewish religion. The writer to the Hebrews, aware of this, lays down his heaviest of the five warnings (Hebrews 5:11—6:20). He explains it with four key concepts.

Key Concept #1: *Know your condition.* You should be taught, but "it is hard to explain because you are slow to learn" (5:11).

If the writer to the Hebrews talked about Melchizedek, these people yawned, "Melchize-who?" If he discussed the priesthood of Jesus, they questioned, "Well, was He related to Aaron?" If he reminded them of their obligation to live right and love God, they responded uneasily, "When is the choir going to sing again?" Any teaching came agonizingly slow because they were sluggish in their reaction to Truth.

You should be teachers, but aren't.

"In fact, though by this time you ought to be teachers, you need someone to teach you the elementary truths of God's Word all over again. You need milk, not solid food. Anyone who lives on milk, being still an infant, is not acquainted with the teaching about righteousness. But solid food is for the mature, who by constant use have trained themselves to distinguish good from evil" (5:12-14).

In one sense, we never outgrow our need for milk. Peter agreed: "Like newborn babies, crave pure spiritual milk, so that by it you may grow up in your salvation, now that you have tasted that the

Lord is good" (1 Peter 2:2-3). Peter is talking about our *desire* for truth. We should always go for truth like a baby goes for milk.

But there should come a time when we want to move on to solid food. It's abnormal to be indifferent about our spiritual nutrition. That's why Paul griped, "Brothers, I could not address you as spiritual but as worldly—mere infants in Christ. I gave you milk, not solid food, for you were not yet ready for it. Indeed, you are still not ready" (1 Corinthians 3:1-2).

And the Bible stresses, "Anyone who lives on milk, being still an infant, is not acquainted with the teaching about righteousness" (Hebrews 5:13). There comes a time to grow up, and it's much sooner than most of us assume.

It Seems As Though I Dug This Foundation Before

When I was in high school, several members of our church youth group decided it would be classy to erect a brick barbecue on the church lawn. Our first goal: a concrete foundation.

We dug down a few inches and made a beautiful hole in the dirt. In that beautiful hole, we put heavy wire mesh with steel rods. No tree roots were going to crack our concrete slab.

Then we poured the concrete and went to work with our tools. Before it dried, we wrote our youth group's initials on it and dated it.
Completed: one nifty foundation.

We bought bricks for the barbecue itself. Someone arranged for the construction of a metal box and the grill mechanism. And we waited for the right time to build.

Now, 10 years later, the concrete slab keeps what will probably be an eternal vigil over a quiet, shaded lawn in the back of a small church in Southern California. Next to it sits a pile of cracked bricks. A fitting introduction to:

Key Concept #2: *Accept the challenge. Go on to maturity.*

"Therefore let us leave the elementary teachings about Christ and go on to maturity. Let us not lay again the foundation of repentance from acts that lead to death, and of faith in God, instruction about baptisms, the laying on of hands, the resurrection of the dead, and eternal judgment. And God permitting, we will do so" (Hebrews 6:1-3).

Not content to bottle-feed spiritual milk to the Hebrew Christians, the writer challenges them to chew on solid food. It's as though the writer stands on the edge of that concrete slab and says, "Stop playing around and rearranging the bricks. Get on with the construction!"

In this section, there are three pairs of elementary teachings:

1. Repentance and faith. Maturity involves going beyond a conversion experience. It's great to become a Christian; it's essential. But it's just a great *beginning.* New life is for living.

2. Instruction about baptisms and laying on of hands. Maturity involves going beyond ceremonies and laws. After the beginning, there should be progress and involvement in the life of the church. This progress should lead to more growth, not to stagnant self-satisfaction.

3. Resurrection of the dead and eternal judgment. Ah! As important as theology is, maturity in-

volves going beyond doctrinal discussions and religious facts.

The author is assuming these Hebrew Christians will, God permitting, go beyond the foundation (6:3). But what if they don't? What if they examine the slab they have been camping on and decide to run away from it, rather than build on it?

What's left if you reject Christ and run recklessly back into the Wilderness of Death?

Free-Fall into Perdition

I am afraid for the person who has been confronted with God's One Final Blazing Word and has hesitated, glaring at it in curiosity, but then turned away, I think of Peter's comment:

"If they have escaped the corruption of the world by knowing our Lord and Saviour Jesus Christ and are again entangled in it and overcome, they are worse off at the end than they were at the beginning. It would have been better for them not to have known the way of righteousness, than to have known it and then to turn their backs on the sacred commandment that was passed on to them. Of them the proverbs are true: 'A dog returns to its vomit,' and, 'A sow that is washed goes back to her wallowing in the mud' " (2 Peter 2:20-22).

And this is part of the warning in Hebrews: "It is impossible for those who have once been enlightened, who have tasted the heavenly gift, who have shared in the Holy Spirit, who have tasted the goodness of the Word of God and the powers of the coming age, if they fall away, to be brought back to repentance, because to their loss they are crucifying the Son of God all over again and subjecting

Him to public disgrace" (Hebrews 6:4-6).

Just how, serious would it have been for these Jewish Christians to abandon Jesus and slip back into Old Testament religion without Him? After all, if they would only reject the Son, the persecution they faced would go away. But if they'd reject the only Way to life, nothing would be left except a terrifying free-fall into absolute destruction.

"Land that drinks in the rain often falling on it and that produces a crop useful to those who farm it receives the blessing of God. But land that produces thorns and thistles is worthless and is in danger of being cursed. In the end it will be burned" (Hebrews 6:7-8).

Better Things in Your Case

I wrote the story of one man's dramatic conversion experience. It had been a sudden and complete change of life — the kind that Christians cheer. Unfortunately, by the time the story came out, he had turned his back on Jesus.

When I hear of people, particularly friends, who have left their commitment to the Son, a few key Bible passages come to mind. One of them: "Being confident of this, that He who began a good work in you will carry it on to completion until the day of Christ Jesus" (Philippians 1:6). When God begins to change a person's life, He wants to complete the job, and He will, unless that person keeps turning his back on God.

But there is another key Bible passage I remember. "Do not be deceived: God cannot be mocked. A man reaps what he sows. The one who sows to please his sinful nature, from that nature will reap

destruction; the one who sows to please the Spirit, from the Spirit will reap eternal life" (Galatians 6:7-8). Eternity is not something to tinker with.

A third Bible passage that I consider when I hear that someone is wavering in his commitment to the Son presents:

Key Concept #3: *Live up to the conviction.*

"Even though we speak like this, dear friends, we are confident of better things in your case — things that accompany salvation. God is not unjust; He will not forget your work and the love you have shown Him as you have helped His people and continue to help them. We want each of you to show this same diligence to the very end, in order to make your hope sure. We do not want you to become lazy, but to imitate those who through faith and patience inherit what has been promised" (Hebrews 6:9-12).

I have had people ask, "How can I know that I am a Christian? I have accepted Jesus as Saviour, but I am just not sure I'm saved." I have considered it vital to turn to 1 John 1:9 and affirm God's forgiveness, but I have also concluded that it's dangerous to go too far in assuring an unsure person that he is a Christian. Maybe he isn't.

New life comes through simple faith, it's true. But some people, who were assured they were right with God, never really trusted the Lord.

Some who think they're Christians should worry when they read the warnings in the Book of Hebrews. It is not enough to trust some vague religious experience: "I walked an aisle" or "I raised my hand" or "I said, 'Yes.'"

So what should give us assurance that we really are Christians? How can we know? *If we're genuine*

*we can count on the Lord to help us live up to what
we believe.*

The serious warning (6:4-8) is followed by: "We
are confident of better things in your case — things
that accompany salvation."

The writer talks about the *past performance* of
the Hebrew Christians (6:10). God will not forget
your work and love, he told them.

But the writer didn't stop there. He gave a *future challenge* (6:11-12). Keep up the good work.
Don't get lazy. "Show this same diligence to the
very end, in order to make your hope sure" (6:11).
Believing in God's Son is no ground for spiritual inactivity (6:12).

Many people offer others assurance of salvation
by reading: "I write these things to you who believe in the name of the Son of God so that you may
know that you have eternal life" (1 John 5:13). Not
"think," not "hope," but *know*, they assure.

But when John said *these things*, what did he
mean? Read 1 John, and discover! A life of godli-
ness is the real proof of salvation, not some feeling
in your "heart." Your heart can fool you (Jeremiah
17:9).

An Anchor, Not a Fluke

A legitimate question may be, *Will we follow
through on our commitments to the Son?*

But there is no question that God will keep His
end of the deal. His faithfulness is seen in:

Key Concept #4: *Receive God's comfort.*

God was faithful to Abraham. "When God made
His promise to Abraham, since there was no one
greater for Him to swear by, He swore by Himself,

saying, 'I will surely bless you and give you many descendants.' And so after waiting patiently, Abraham received what was promised" (Hebrews 6:13-15). God made a promise and kept His Word.

God will fulfill His promise to us. He wanted to make clear to us that His purpose would not change. So, in addition to the promise, He gave an oath (6:16-17). God has great plans for our eternity and He wants us to know that He will fulfill His promise, if we keep our end of the deal. "God did this so that, by two unchangeable things [His promise and His oath] in which it is impossible for God to lie, we who have fled to take hold of the hope offered to us may be greatly encouraged" (6:18).

Besides these examples of God's faithfulness, we also know *God's Son represents us.* "We have this hope as an anchor for the soul, firm and secure. It enters the inner sanctuary behind the curtain, where Jesus, who went before us, has entered on our behalf. He has become a High Priest forever, just like Melchizedek" (6:19-20).

Left to ourselves, we're nothing but parched earth. If we go our own ways, God's seed will only bear thorns and thistles. But once the Sonshine penetrates us, new life sprouts out of the parched earth.

Slowly, Prodigal sensed a change. Before, the Sonshine had terrified him. The heat had seemed unbearable, the Light intense. Now Prodigal was beginning to feel the subtle difference between scorching heat and healing warmth.

As Prodigal's eyes continued to adjust to the blazing Sonshine, he realized for the first time that living Light not only exposes weakness. It also brings understanding.

Remembering the small, leather-bound Book in his backpack, Prodigal pulled it out and began to read. He turned the pages deliberately, studying each one as if he had all the time he needed.

Then he read, "Sonshine never sets. It is merely eclipsed by mutiny. In all time," the Book continued, "there was one 'total eclipse' that lasted three days, but conquered darkness forever."

Prodigal toyed with his growing understanding.

6

What we desperately need is a Force outside us
strong enough to overpower us—One Final
Blazing Word to melt our resistance. Yet that
Force must also be a permanent Friend who
sticks with us and helps us. What we need is . . .

The Invasion
of the Son-Word

I cross Sixth Street to the Los Angeles bus depot,
jostled by the crowd. The sun is bright, the colors
vivid, but I feel depressed. *The people are so cold
they might as well be machines* I think. *Including
me.*

I reach the corner and the signal cautions me,
"Don't Walk." So I spend the moment comparing.
The traffic on the sidewalks and the traffic on the
streets seem so similar, so mechanical. Am I seeing
both the cars and the people as machines?

When I pass through the depot's glass double
doors, the brightness fades. Suddenly, everything is
institutional gray. I wait for my eyes to adjust to the
darkness, then make my way through the nameless
crowd to the proper line where I'll wait my turn for
a ticket.

Then, two lines over, I recognize a face. *It's*

Dave, I'm sure it is, though I haven't seen him since our school days together. I leave my place in line, step around some suitcases and call out, "Hey, Dave! It's Jim. How are ya doin', man?"

I identify myself because Dave is blind. As a child he listened to his folks fight and somehow concluded he was the reason. He tried, unsuccessfully, to take his life, losing his eyesight in the process.

Dave strains to hear what I'm saying. I notice that he has a hearing aid. Then his face brightens in recognition. We talk about what we've been doing since high school.

At first, Dave's story horrifies me. While in college, he discovered that he had a brain tumor. The doctors at UCLA Medical Center operated immediately, but the tumor had already done a lot of damage. As a result, Dave lost much of his senses of hearing, taste, smell, and even touch. *Losing contact with the world,* I think. *How awful.*

But Dave is cheerful. He goes on to tell me how another college student took a special interest in him during his illness. This friend told Dave about Jesus' love, and the joy of being a child of God. Dave chose to become a Christian!

"I'm blind physically, and that's bad," Dave explains. "But for years I was blind spiritually, and that was much worse!"

Jesus amazes me! He not only changed David. He's also changed me. And I reflect: A changed life is the mark that God's One Final Blazing Word has been given in a unique way to the world He created.

So the birth of Jesus was a worldwide, timeless Invasion of the Son-Word. Today that "Friendly Invasion" becomes personal to those who trust the

Son, the Word. And that Word brings change.

For example: Saul, the militant, marched off on an anti-Christian mission, determined to darken the Son. But on the Damascus Road, he encountered that Son, blazing in fury but glowing in grace. Saul of Tarsus became the Apostle Paul. He was changed. Radically. The Son-Word invaded his life.

The Son's invasion is a great conquest of love and holiness. Today He invades with forgiveness. But someday, when He returns, He'll invade with judgment. So we should accept His Friendly Invasion gratefully.

The Son-Word is liberating, so we can welcome and accept His friendship and His lordship. God's One Final Blazing Word can melt our resistance.

But What about This Priesthood?

The writer to the Hebrews refers to Jesus as our Great High Priest. "He had to be made like His brothers in every way, in order that He might become a merciful and faithful High Priest in service to God" (2:17).

But, these skeptical Hebrew Christians may have thought, *priests come from the tribe of Levi. Jesus is from the tribe of Judah. How on earth could Jesus be a priest? And a Great High Priest at that?*

Anticipating that question, the writer says, "No one takes this honor [of being a priest] on himself; he must be called by God, just as Aaron was. So Christ also did not take on Himself the glory of becoming a High Priest. But God said to Him, 'You are My Son; today I have become Your Father.' And He says in another place, 'You are a Priest forever, in the order of Melchizedek' " (5:4-6).

Jesus, then, is not like a Levitical priest; He is not like Aaron. He is a priest like Melchizedek. But what does all this mean?

The Next Logical Question

Who is this Melchizedek? And how is Jesus like Him?

"This Melchizedek was king of Salem and priest of God Most High. He met Abraham returning from the defeat of the kings and blessed him, and Abraham gave him a tenth of everything. First, [Melchizedek's] name means 'king of righteousness'; then also, 'king of Salem' means 'king of peace.' Without father or mother ... without beginning of days or end of life, like the Son of God he remains a priest forever' " (7:1-3).

Melchizedek is mentioned only twice in the Old Testament. He was mentioned in Psalm 110 which is quoted several times in Hebrews, "The Lord has sworn and will not change His mind: 'You are a Priest forever, in the order of Melchizedek' " (110:4).

We get a bit more insight into Melchizedek in Genesis 14:18-20. Abraham had been concerned about the welfare of his nephew Lot who had been captured. Abraham tore out in hot pursuit, routed Lot's captors, rescued Lot, and seized a lot of booty. As Abraham was returning, he met Melchizedek, the king-priest. Melchizedek pronounced a blessing on Abraham.

We begin to see why Jesus is compared to Melchizedek. Melchizedek was both a king and a priest. So is Jesus. Melchizedek was the king of righteousness and the king of peace—both appropriate titles for Jesus. Melchizedek came on the scene in Genesis with no record of father or mother, with no reference in Scripture to his birth or death. He's the closest picture we have of an eternal king-priest—before Jesus.

A Better Priest Than Levi

"But," the Hebrew Christian might have persisted, "when it comes to priests, how can we do better than Levi?"

For starters, *Melchizedek was greater than Abraham.*

"Just think how great he was: Even the patriarch Abraham gave him a tenth of the plunder! Now the law requires the descendants of Levi who become priests to collect a tenth from the people—that is, their brothers—even though their brothers are descended from Abraham. This man, however, did not trace his descent from Levi; yet he collected a tenth from Abraham and blessed him who had the promises. And without doubt the lesser person is blessed by the greater" (Hebrews 7:4-7).

The Levitical priesthood regulation about tithing (giving a tenth of a person's earnings) didn't exist at the time of Abraham. In spite of that, Abraham paid tithes to Melchizedek. Obviously, then, Melchizedek was greater than Abraham.

So what?

So *if Melchizedek was greater than Abraham, he's also greater than Levi.*

"In the one case, the tenth is collected by men who die; but in the other case, by him who is declared to be living. One might even say that Levi, who collects the tenth, paid the tenth through Abraham, because when Melchizedek met Abraham, Levi was still in the body of his ancestor" (7:8-10).

In paying tithes to Melchizedek, Abraham was acting as a representative of all his descendants. It is as if Levi had paid tithes to Melchizedek—as if Levi had said, "Melchizedek is greater than I."

So what?

So *if Melchizedek's priesthood is greater than Levi's, then the priesthood of Jesus is also greater.*

Power in the Priesthood

I'm always amazed at the power that Jesus, our Priest, can have in lives. I remember one church service in which an elderly man spoke. He'd been a gunslinger during the sunset years of the real wild West. Later he'd been a thief and a hit man.

Then, as a spunky old man, he turned to Jesus. His hardness and cruelty melted as he, through faith, experienced the Friendly Invasion of the Son-Word. His trust in Jesus mellowed him and changed the pattern of his life. The Force that ultimately overpowered him stayed with him as a permanent Friend.

"If perfection could have been attained through the Levitical priesthood (for on the basis of it the Law was given to the people), why was there still need for another priest to come—one in the order of Melchizedek, not in the order of Aaron? For when there is a change of the priesthood, there must also be a change of the Law. He of whom these things are said belonged to a different tribe, and no one from that tribe has ever served at the altar. For it is clear that our Lord descended from Judah, and in regard to that tribe Moses said nothing about priests" (Hebrews 7:11-14).

The priesthood of Jesus is unique. It accomplishes, thanks to Jesus' great sacrifice, what Levi's priesthood couldn't accomplish. And, whereas Levi's priesthood was temporary, Jesus' priesthood is forever.

The Indestructible Life

Indestructible. That's the guarantee we need. The old *temporary* Levi priesthood has been replaced by the new *permanent* priesthood of Jesus. His priesthood will never change hands; it will never become obsolete.

"And what we have said is even more clear if another Priest like Melchizedek appears, One who has become a Priest not on the basis of a regulation as to His ancestry but on the basis of the power of an indestructible life. For it is declared: 'You are a Priest forever, just like Melchizedek.' The former regulation is set aside because it was weak and useless (for the Law made nothing perfect), and a better hope is introduced, by which we draw near to God" (7:15-19).

Even death couldn't put this Priest out of commission. The enormous Easter tombstone was rolled away. The Son's short stay with death ended. Forever.

Compared with Jesus' priesthood, Levi's was weak and useless. It could make nothing perfect. But Jesus' priesthood introduced a better hope for us all.

Yet Levi's priesthood accomplished precisely

what was intended: It pointed the way to that better hope.

"If a law had been given that could impart life, then righteousness would certainly have come by the Law. But the Scripture declares that the whole world is a prisoner of sin, so that what was promised, being given through faith in Jesus Christ, might be given to those who believe.

"Before this faith came, we were held prisoners by the Law, locked up until faith should be revealed. So the Law was put in charge to lead us to Christ that we might be justified by faith. Now that faith has come, we are no longer under the supervision of the Law" (Galatians 3:21-25).

The Unchangeable System

Jesus, the indestructible Son-Word, is our guarantee that our own new life isn't temporary. The changes He makes in a new life are only the beginning. God has given His word.

"And it was not without an oath! Others became priests without any oath, but He became a Priest with an oath when God said to Him: 'The Lord has sworn and will not change His mind, "You are a Priest forever."' Because of this oath, Jesus has become the guarantee of a better covenant" (Hebrews 7:20-22).

This must have been a staggering thought to people who were used to thinking of priests in strictly human terms. If your church has had a rapid turnover of pastors you can appreciate what the writer of Hebrews is saying.

OK, so maybe the Old Testament priests had longer terms of service. Still you see personnel changes. When one died, a new man took over. But with the priesthood of Jesus, things have changed. The temporary has been put aside, and Jesus will be our priest forever.

"Now there were many of those priests, since death prevented them from continuing in office; but because Jesus lives forever, He has a permanent priesthood. Therefore He is able to save completely those who come to God through Him, because He always lives to intercede for them" (Hebrews 7:23-25).

The Priest We Need

What is it that draws people to Jesus, that makes them willing to tear down their defenses and eagerly give in to the Friendly Invasion of the Son-Word? It's exhilarating to watch the process as God's One Final Blazing Word melts the resistance in a person, then quietly, lovingly invades his life.

Ed was a burly man who worked for a trucking firm in Los Angeles. Rose, his quiet, submissive, unassuming wife, constantly affirmed her love for him. They'd previously been exposed to the Gospel and had been somewhat interested. But then came that unforgettable moment when the Son-Word melted all their resistance and they became joyful Christians.

They were active for a time, eager to follow through with their new commitments. But then they wavered.

We need, it seems, a continual melting of resistance, a willing surrender of all our life's territory to the Friendly Invasion. Nothing will diminish the work of the Son. But with our own openness, we must meet His determination to change us. That's not hard when we consider Him:

"Such a High Priest meets our need—One who is holy, blameless, pure, set apart from sinners, exalted above the heavens. Unlike the other high priests, He does not need to offer sacrifices day after day, first for His own sins, and then for the sins of the people. He sacrificed for their sins once and for all when He offered Himself. For the Law appoints as high priests men who are weak; but the oath, which came after the Law, appointed the Son, who has been made perfect forever" (Hebrews 7:26-28).

Still grasping the leather-bound Book, Prodigal turned to face the Sonshine. His thoughts whirled. Something deep inside him cautioned, *Sonshine should be feared.* Yet that dark thought was instantly overpowered.

Prodigal took one step toward the Son. Immediately Sonshine loomed closer, larger than any sun he had ever seen. Pulsating waves of heat and light crashed against him like roaring surf. A penetrating warmth drenched his consciousness.

Prodigal recalled that certain conclusion: *I cannot leave this Light and live. But if I stay I am sure that I must die.* Now he wondered. Just what would die? His personality? His happiness? Or would this Sonshine consume his fears, his mutiny, his dark, questionable values?

There is no restful warmth without blistering heat. The words shot through him, penetrating every dark hole of his life. The Son before him was now enormous and still growing, beckoning. Prodigal could no longer distinguish the Son and sky from the horizon; everything was living Light. He stripped off his cumbersome backpack and tossed it to the ground. Then, clutching his leather-bound Book, he ran westward into the Sonshine itself.

He felt a blast of blistering heat and knew that Sonshine was consuming his darkest thoughts and fears. He did not slacken his pace. Each stride brought him miles into the expanse of Sonshine until he was surrounded by a glowing, healing warmth.

This, he told himself, *is how truth feels.*

7

It is not enough to have outward rules to live by, a moral code to follow. The Son-Word Himself must penetrate the fiber of our lives if we are to live in . . .

The Cosmic Dimension

The drummer was still setting up when the guitarists and bass player began moving through their warm-up chords. It was then that it occurred to Bob that he just couldn't sing.

He disconnected the mikes, apologized to the stunned group, and left.

Before John was 14 years old, he'd lived in 16 different foster homes. He'd learned how to con people. A little whining around and he got what he wanted. He fought his way through school and became bitter. He didn't think anyone cared about him, and he didn't care about anyone else. All John wanted to be was a Hell's Angel.

Finally, something changed his life.

Then there's Roy. His mother died when he was two. His dad sent him to Oklahoma to live with his grandparents. When his dad remarried, he sent for Roy to return home. But the kind of home and family life Roy expected and hoped for never happened. Instead, Roy was raised in a military academy, away from normal family life.

Yet, as a high school student, a slow change began. Eventually, Roy's entire life was turned around.

Bob, John, and Roy were all changed by Jesus. They all gave in to the Friendly Invasion of the Son-Word. When they did, they discovered life in the Cosmic Dimension. It was not just a one-shot experience, or a religious kick. Jesus, the Son-Word, brought with Him a radically new outlook for their lives. It was more than a new moral code or a set of religious rules to follow blindly. These three people, and thousands like them, discovered a whole new motivation that can enter a life, penetrating every part, changing desires, bringing a Cosmic Dimension.

Let me illustrate from the experiences of Bob, John, and Roy.

Bob's goal had been to be a hit in the secular music world. As he became a Christian, his desires began to change. He developed a new outlook.

A couple days after becoming a Christian he went to band practice. Then for the first time, he began to understand:

"We were getting ready to set up and were working on this one song—I don't even remember what it was—but as we started going through the chords, it occurred to me that the song was dirty.

"And that was just one of the songs that really bothered me. I decided that I just couldn't be a Christian and do this kind of music."

Where did Bob get his new outlook?

John's rough background left deep impressions on him. The man who told him about Jesus had just helped him fix his motorcycle. But John became impatient about the direction their conversation was taking and he exploded.

"I'm gonna break your jaw," John shot at him. "I believe the Bible, but don't mess up my life."

Soon the tough-guy image broke and John surrendered his life to Jesus. For years John had been intensely self-involved. But then he began investing his life in others.

Where did John get his new outlook?

Roy had not learned firsthand how to be tender, how to care for others. He grew up having to obey strict rules. Roy learned many of life's lessons from bathroom graffiti and locker room conversation. Even after becoming a Christian, improving his self-image was a long, uphill struggle.

"I guess athletics became a substitute family for me. Even after the military academy, my home life didn't amount to much. We didn't know one another. I had a hard time getting along with other guys my age too, because I'd never liked myself."

As it turned out, Roy graduated from high school with a number of athletic scholarships to choose from. Eventually, he passed up all of them for a different vocation, using his energy to serve others.

Where did Roy get his new outlook?

The Cosmic Life-giver

Bob, John, and Roy are all involved full-time in sharing the Christian message, spreading the Friendly Invasion of the Son-Word. They discovered that Jesus could give life a fresh perspective, a Cosmic Dimension. Their experiences are evidence that God kept a special Old Testament promise. We have a perfect High Priest who has introduced a new agreement.

"The point of what we are saying is this: We do have such a High Priest, who sat down at the right hand of the throne of the Majesty in heaven, and who serves in the sanctuary, the true tabernacle set up by the Lord, not by man" (Hebrews 8:1-2).

In the past few chapters, we looked at this High Priest, Jesus. Now the point is flatly stated: "We do have such a High Priest." We have a Representative who understands our frustrations perfectly and is in a position to help us. He is active, serving in this Great Galactic Sanctuary "set up by the Lord, not by man." Jesus, God's One Final Blazing Word, is our own Representative, speaking for us in heaven.

Jesus' own followers, to say nothing of His enemies, had a hard time accepting Him as who He claimed to be. They could not understand this mysterious Man. When He multiplied a young lad's brown-bag lunch and fed a hungry crowd of 5,000 men—plus women and children—they were ready to make Him king. Had Jesus *been* the *physical* king or priest they wanted, they would have followed Him as long as He kept performing the flashy miracles they wanted.

But Jesus said, "Do not work for food that spoils, but for food that endures to eternal life" (John 6:27).

Paul said that what God wants to communicate is a secret hidden wisdom. "None of the rulers of this age understood it," he said, "for if they had, they would not have crucified the Lord of glory" (1 Corinthians 2:8).

People took as concrete reality what God intended to be a mere shadow which reflected a greater reality. For example, earthly priests were to be shadows, reflecting the Great High Priest, Jesus. And the earthly tabernacle was merely a shadow, reflecting heaven.

Beyond the Shadow

The Greek philosopher Plato liked to explain his concept of reality with a story. It was as if, Plato said, a man were sitting in front of a fire in a cave gazing at the shadows cast on the stone walls. These shadows were all he knew of reality.

One day the man ventured out to the mouth of the cave. He stepped into the blazing brilliance of the sunlight. But it was too overpowering. The man squinted, covered his eyes, and ultimately returned to the inner recesses of the dark cave. There, "reality" was comfortable.

You might say the Jews were in a religious cave, attached to their shadowy religion. Few ever saw the Sonshine beyond it.

Hebrews contrasts Jesus, the Sonshine of God, with the shadows of Jewish religion.

"But the ministry Jesus has received is as superior to theirs as the covenant of which He is Mediator is superior to the old one, and it is founded on better promises" (Hebrews 8:6).

Actually, everyone has a shadowy cave he calls reality or truth. But when he opens himself to the Friendly Invasion of the Son-Word, darkness dissolves into blazing Sonshine. Life takes on a Cosmic Dimension.

Better Promises, Another Deal

If we cling to shadows, we're captivated rather than liberated. We should be able to run free in the Sonshine of God, not sit imprisoned in a dark cave. Man-made religions and rules bring death. Trying to follow moral codes doesn't really break habits or replace wrong desires with good ones. Trying to improve by ourselves ends in frustration, even if we appear successful.

For instance, a rich young man ran to Jesus, eager to know the way to eternal life (Mark 10:17-31). "Good Teacher," he asked, "what must I do to inherit eternal life?"

"Why do you call Me good?" Jesus answered. "No one is good—except God alone."

I suspect the young man began to get depressed right then. *No one is good but God.* This rich young man said he'd kept the Ten Commandments. But he lacked one thing—right values. *No one is good but God.* The only hope for a new, changed life is a new agreement—better promises. "For if there had been nothing wrong with that first covenant, no place would have been sought for another. But God found fault with the people" (Hebrews 8:7-8).

Actually, the first covenant did just what God intended: It served as a shadow pointing to the New Covenant; it showed people their need, their own inabilities. The problem was that the people couldn't keep the covenant.

The Contrast Continues

As the writer to the Hebrews has contrasted incomplete revelations of God with His One Final

Blazing Word, he now contrasts the old and new covenants. As Jesus is superior to angels, Moses, and the Old Testament priesthood, the writer now affirms Jesus' new covenant is superior to the old.

" 'The time is coming,' declares the Lord, 'when I will make a New Covenant with the house of Israel and with the house of Judah. It will not be like the covenant I made with their forefathers when I took them by the hand to lead them out of Egypt, because they did not remain faithful to My covenant, and I turned away from them' " (8:8-9). In spite of Israel's failure to keep the first covenant, God still promised a new covenant. God made that promise through Jeremiah after the 10 Northern Tribes (Israel) had already been taken captive by Assyria (Jeremiah 31:31). As for the 2 Southern Tribes (Judah), the Babylonians had almost completed their work destroying them.

At this low point in the Jews' history, God gave hope. He cared about the people as a nation. It grieved Him that they were divided and politically destroyed. He promised a covenant, ultimately to be kept with both Israel and Judah. Someday they would be politically reunited and be given new life.

But God's concern was not merely national or political. He had a deeper individual concern. God had led the Jews out of Egypt years earlier and had made that first covenant agreement with them. No sooner had the Law been given than Israel had disobeyed. The result: 40 years of wandering in the desert. Then, even after being established in the land God had promised Israel, the Jews turned their backs on God and broke the covenant. The nation was divided and destroyed.

God's New Covenant would be different. It would remove the problem of individual rebellion. God would crush the mutiny in His followers from the inside out by placing His Law within them. The days of external regulation would be put aside. The shadows would dissolve into the Sonshine of reality. There would be a Friendly Invasion of the Son-Word. Life would take on a Cosmic Dimension.

Today, by trusting Jesus, we can experience the Friendly Invasion of the Son-Word. He begins the lifelong process of changing our habits, actions, and thoughts. He redirects our values, goals, and desires. We get a taste of what it will be like to live forever in the Cosmic Dimension.

A Promise of Invasion

Think again of Bob, John, and Roy. What was it that changed them? Bob had met a friend whose life was different. It was an enjoyable difference, not a stuffy difference. He stopped resisting. Then his life was changed, gradually but soundly. The difference was real and enjoyable.

John's hardened, self-sufficient facade crumbled when he was forced to take an honest look at himself. First he accepted Jesus. Then the change came—like a snake shedding its skin. Layer after layer of the old life dropped off and was replaced by new values and attitudes.

Roy's military academy experience included a conversation with a chaplain who shared the story of the change Jesus made in his life. He took a personal interest in Roy and showed him that Christianity makes sense. Being a part of God's family was inviting to Roy. He accepted, and a new Force entered his life; God's principles entered and changed his life.

The new covenant involves individual lives being changed from the inside out. But it promises more than that. It is bigger still, with three guarantees.

Guarantee # 1: *God will put His wisdom inside His followers.* The time of external rules is over.

" 'This is the covenant I will make with the house of Israel after that time,' declares the Lord. 'I will put My laws in their minds and write them on their hearts. I will be their God, and they will be My people' " (Hebrews 8:10).

God's first covenant did not *guarantee* that people would have right desires, though many of the Lord's followers did. This New Covenant offers the hope of right desires. God Himself promises to change the lives of people, not by a code of morals or outward rules, but from the inside.

Guarantee 2: *Everyone accepting the new covenant will have this personal knowledge of God.*

"No longer will a man teach his neighbor, or a man his brother, saying, 'Know the Lord,' because they will all know Me, from the least of them to the greatest" (8:11).

Under the Old Covenant there was no *guarantee* that a person would have an individual relationship with God. Priests and prophets were constantly sharing the Word of the Lord, encouraging people to "know Him." Under the New Covenant, *all* of God's people will know Him personally, not just priests and prophets.

Guarantee #3: *God will give complete forgiveness to everyone taking part in the New Covenant.*

"I will forgive their wickedness and will remember their sins no more" (8:12).

Under the Old Covenant, God offered forgiveness to people who were truly sorry for their sins. Still, they lived in the shadow. Repeated bloody

animal sacrifices were constant reminders that a
perfect sacrifice had not yet been given. Then God
gave His One Final Blazing Word, and our sin was
paid for, without our having to sacrifice or be
punished for our own sins.

The National Dimension

So what about the Jew who still looked for a mate-
rial kingdom? What about all the promises God
made to Israel?

When Jesus returns, He will be coming to make
good some yet-unfulfilled promises. The three
guarantees of the New Covenant relate not only to
Christians, but also many Jews. He will put His laws
inside them; they will have personal knowledge of
God; as a nation their sins will be forgiven. This is a
big part of the reality the Old Covenant was pointing to. The Book of Revelation, difficult as it is to
understand, gives much of the background of that
future time. The Lord will return in judgment and
then will rule over a literal kingdom. Israel will
play a big part in that. An ultimate fulfillment of
the New Covenant is coming.

"By calling this covenant 'new,' He has made the
first one obsolete; and what is obsolete and aging
will soon disappear" (Hebrews 8:13).

From Prodigal's new vantage point in the core of the Sonshine, he realized that he now saw things quite differently than before. He looked behind him through the ages and noticed shadows that, until now, he had taken for granted. Many of the things he saw only partially before he now saw completely.

Before, it had almost seemed that everything was covered with darkness. What little Light he recognized had seemed inappropriate, something to be feared. He now comprehended that the Light was normal, even healthy, and that darkness was the unfortunate consequence of some strange mutiny. And yet, he could also see that even the dark places had some puzzling purpose. It was as if the shadows were large directional arrows pointing toward the Son.

He turned from his view of the past and looked once again ahead of him—ages ahead of him. As he did, he saw not only the Sonshine that surrounded him, but he began to see other things. Wonderful things. And desolating things.

8

It is only as we see all the ages through the Son that they become understandable. Only then do we see truth rising . . .

Up from the Shadows

For a small community college it wasn't half bad: situated atop a hill, adjoining a large cemetery (quiet neighbors), overlooking a dairy farm . . . and, on clear days, the entire Los Angeles basin. The largest structure was the five-story library.

One particularly stunning spring day, I avoided the elevator and began climbing the outdoor stairs. I think I was on about the third floor when I saw Ted. We had gone to elementary school together, but hadn't seen each other in several years. A lot had happened since then. I had experienced the Friendly Invasion of the Son-Word—I was a Christian. Ted, I wasn't so sure about. I seriously doubted he would have become a Christian, just as I guess others wouldn't have thought that my life had changed.

Something else had happened—earlier that week, in fact. I had been reading the local newspaper and came across an item that had arrested my attention. My elementary school friend, Ted, had approached a railroad crossing. Ignoring the fact that the arms were down, the lights flashing, the bells clanging, Ted had decided to maneuver his Jeep between the barriers and beat the long freight train across. And then, as if a melodramatic pre-talkie movie script had just come to life, the Jeep's engine quit. Ted leaped from the vehicle just in time to watch the freight train flatten his Jeep like an old soup can.

As I had read that news report I had thought, *Wow! Is he ever fortunate!* I reflected, *Wouldn't it be great to have an opportunity to talk to him!* Then, only a few days later, we met on the third floor of the library, at a school I didn't even know he attended.

Weighing my words carefully, I began, "Ted, hey listen, I'm really sorry about what happened with your Jeep! Man, I read that and couldn't help thinking, *What if Ted hadn't made it out?* Say, Ted, I just have to tell you about a change that has taken place in my life...." And I began giving him the story.

As I did, I noticed a dramatic and uneasy change in Ted's expression. It was as if his conscience was sending little signals to him, like a bleeping electronic game, and his mind was reaching for the off switch.

Then, awkwardly, Ted dismissed himself. Something about studying for auto shop comprehensives, I think. Ted walked off and I stood there, on the third floor of the library, reflecting on how very fortunate he was. And how responsible.

Conscience—it's like a small voice that shouts quietly the persistent message: *Something must change!*

It's easy to employ creative tactics to battle a

conscience we do not care to hear. We button it up, try to silence it. We compromise with it, going only so far, but falling short of its demands. We sacrifice to it, a little religion here, a little kindness there.

Conscience is strong, but so is our will. In an out-and-out contest, our willfulness usually wins. We twist our conscience so that the already quiet message is quieter.

God's writer contrasts the old system (God's Old Covenant) with the new Son-Word system (Hebrews 9:1-28). This chapter demonstrates that the connection between the two covenant agreements is like the connection between light and the shadow it casts. This New Covenant agreement, the Son-Word system, is even able to clean up a dirty and defeated conscience. Which shows something of how fortunate *we* are. And how responsible.

Discussing the Undiscussables

The writer sets up that old-system new-system contrast by first discussing some strange-but-purposeful elements of that first covenant.

"Now the first covenant had regulations for worship and also an earthly sanctuary" (9:1).

These regulations for worship were God's idea. He intended this earthly sanctuary and the Old Covenant religious system to point toward a greater heavenly system to come, the Son-Word system. That first covenant and all the elements of worship and sacrifice were designed to show the need for that greater system which would both clear the conscience of the worshiper and make him right with God.

Unfortunately, Israel as a whole did not try too

hard to live up to the Old Covenant. Instead, in an effort to clean up protesting consciences, the Jews merely added traditions and regulations to the original God-given ideas. Jesus sharply condemned this adding to the old system.

"You nullify the Word of God," He said, "for the sake of your tradition. You hypocrites! Isaiah was right when he prophesied about you: 'These people honor Me with their lips, but their hearts are far from Me. They worship Me in vain; their teachings are but rules taught by men' " (Matthew 15:6-9).

Why the man-made additions to God's ideas? At least one reason is a warped response to a screaming conscience. Our conscience tabs us guilty, so we trump up a ton of additional rules. If we keep some of them, we feel more religious; if we don't make it, we feel we've at least attempted the morally impossible.

That's one reason some people are drawn to the cults. Cults offer a conscience-calming system of rules that make you feel so religious, so spiritual, so other-worldly. But God designed His first-covenant religious system to point to the Son, who is its fulfillment—the way to a clear conscience.

Behind the Curtains

The description itself sounds other-worldly, clearly as if it were intended to point to some reality other than itself.

"A tabernacle [tent] was set up. In its first room were the lampstand, the table, and the consecrated bread: this was called the Holy Place" (Hebrews 9:2).

The tent was a handy portable church building that the nation of Israel used as it wandered in the desert. God had given specific directions for the construction of this worship center in Exodus, chapters 25 through 40. It was to be 45 feet long, 15 feet wide, and 15 feet high. The enclosed part of the structure was to be divided into two rooms, filled with furniture and articles of significance to the nation.

"Behind the second curtain was a room called the Most Holy Place, which had the golden altar of incense and the gold-covered Ark of the Covenant. This ark contained the gold jar of manna, Aaron's rod that had budded, and the stone tablets of the covenant. Above the ark were the cherubim of the Glory, overshadowing the place of atonement. But we cannot discuss these in detail now" (Hebrews 9:3-5).

Though the Old Testament priests often entered the outer room, the Holy Place, the *Most* Holy Place was entered only once a year and only by the high priest. He entered this room to observe certain sacred rituals on the Day of Atonement, a day set aside each year to remind people of a future time when badness and moral dirt would be permanently cleaned up by a Great High Priest, God's One Final Blazing Word.

External, Internal, Ceremony, Truth

Rather than a detailed discussion of budding rods, cherubim and glory, the writer moves on toward the contrast.

"When everything had been arranged like this, the priests entered regularly into the outer room to carry on their ministry. But only the high priest entered the inner room, and that only once a year, and never without blood, which he offered for himself and for the sins the people had committed in ignorance" (Hebrews 9:6-7).

The importance of the blood, admittedly a gruesome thought, is explained later. But first, the bigger picture:

"The Holy Spirit was showing by this that the way into the Most Holy Place had not yet been disclosed as long as the first tabernacle was still standing" (9:8).

This was the point that had been missed. The tent, the lampstand, the stone tablets, the budding rod, they all were intended to point to something greater: a New Covenant—the Son-Word system, God's One Final Blazing Word, a Friendly Invasion into willing lives, life in a Cosmic Dimension.

"This is an illustration for the present time, indicating that the gifts and sacrifices being offered were not able to clear the conscience of the worshiper. They are only a matter of food and drink and various ceremonial washings—external regulations applying until the time of the new order" (Hebrews 9:9-10).

Please Frame My Reference

While in college, I worked for a while for a tool company. This proved an unusual experience for several reasons, but chiefly because few of the employees spoke English. It is indeed an odd experience to ask someone a question and for a response get only a broad toothy grin. It is likewise a weird sensation to be asked a question and realize you can do little more than flash a broad toothy grin.

Even so, some of the biggest communication breakdowns came while communicating with people who spoke our own language. "Mark," the foreman said, "don't bring the forklift in here. Too crowded." Ten minutes later Mark came chugging in, determined to show off his remarkable ability to handle the machine. *Crunch!* One of the forks caught a table leg and busted it off. The table collapsed and, with it, several hundred tool cases that had been sorted, counted, and piled there. The rest of us laughed . . . in the same language.

Let that stand as an illustration of the Old Covenant and people's failure to understand it. Sure, the concepts were then new—different, unusual, foreign, even other-worldly. But even in those instances where it was understood, pride and disobedience took over. The results were disastrous.

The first covenant with its strange regulations would have been valueless if Old Testament worshipers had not seen beyond the forms to the deeper message they foreshadowed.

"When Christ came as High Priest of the good things that are already here, He went through the greater and more perfect tabernacle that is not man-made, that is to say, not a part of this creation. He did not enter by means of the blood of goats and calves, but He entered the Most Holy Place once for all by His own blood, having obtained eternal redemption" (Hebrews 9:11-12).

But It All Sounds So Repulsive!

"Oh," a disgusted relative shot back, "Christianity is a slaughterhouse religion. All that blood!"

That comment stopped me. I just did not know how to respond.

I suppose I had focused so much on the love and goodness of God that I hadn't stopped to consider just how much writers of the Bible talked about blood. Abraham had even been asked to offer his own son, Isaac—though God did provide an alternative (Genesis 22). Lambs were killed. Blood was splattered on doorposts (Exodus 12). Priests put lamb's blood on people's ears, thumbs, and toes (Leviticus 14). *Blood. Blood. Blood.* My relative was right! And I wondered, *Why all the blood? What's the point?*

Several years later, the first time I read Hebrews 9, I saw at least this much: The prominence of the blood is intentional. That blood was pointing to something greater.

"The blood of goats and bulls and the ashes of a heifer sprinkled on those who are ceremonially unclean sanctify them so that they are outwardly clean. How much more, then, will the blood of Christ, who through the eternal Spirit offered Himself unblemished to God, cleanse our consciences from acts that lead to death, so that we may serve the living God!" (Hebrews 9:13-14)

There is a relationship then between blood—specifically the blood of Jesus—and a person's conscience being clean. Can it be that God chose something as drastic and devastating as the shedding of His Son's blood to show us just how extensive our moral dirt is? Apart from God, we are so twisted and dead that it took the execution of Jesus to straighten us and give us life.

"For this reason Christ is the Mediator of a New Covenant, that those who are called may receive the promised eternal inheritance—now that He has died as a ransom to set them free from the sins committed under the first covenant" (Hebrews 9:15).

Will Typed in Blood

As I now reflect on that conversation with my relative, I wonder, *Did she realize just how much emphasis is placed on the blood?* Repulsive as it may seem, you cannot take the blood out of Christianity and keep it as Christianity. The two are tied—inseparably so.

Christians, people who have received the Friendly Invasion of the Son-Word, have been named heirs in a will typed in blood. We have a costly inheritance.

"In the case of a will," the writer to the Hebrews continues, "it is necessary to prove the death of the one who made it, because a will is in force only when somebody has died; it never takes effect while the one who made it is living" (Hebrews 9:16-17).

And what about the blood?

"This is why even the first covenant was not put into effect without blood. When Moses had proclaimed every commandment of the Law to all the people, he took the blood of calves, together with water, scarlet wool, and branches of hyssop, and sprinkled the scroll and all the people.

"He said, 'This is the blood of the covenant, which God has commanded you to keep.' In the same way, he sprinkled with the blood both the tabernacle and everything used in its ceremonies.

"In fact, [and here the point is clearly stated] the Law requires that nearly everything be cleansed with blood, and without the shedding of blood there is no forgiveness" (Hebrews 9:18-22).

It shouldn't be too shocking then that Jesus, the night before His execution, had something to say about blood. Before His perplexed followers, He lifted a cup of wine and said, "This cup is the New Covenant in My blood" (1 Corinthians 11:25).

Even today, as we observe the Lord's Supper, we are acting out a drama to remind one another that our inheritance as Christians was costly. The will was typed in blood. Jesus' death was gruesome; our gory guarantee of heaven. "Without the shedding of blood there is no forgiveness" (Hebrews 9:22b).

Pure Shadows Clean Light

I think again of my conversation with my friend, Ted, as we stood on the third floor balcony of the college library. My mention of Jesus. His nervous response. Then I had wondered, *Was I clear enough in my explanation?* Anyone who understood would surely respond.

And I consider: God spent centuries preparing the people of this planet for the great unveiling of His One Final Blazing Word. He gave us an elaborate shadow-picture to prepare people for that blazing light. Still, people squinted against its brightness and turned away. Only those who would look up from the shadows and into the Son could see and comprehend.

"It was necessary, then, for the copies of the heavenly things to be purified with these sacrifices [the blood of calves, etc.], but the heavenly things themselves with better sacrifices than these. For Christ did not enter a man-made sanctuary that was only a copy of the true one; He entered heaven itself, now to appear for us in God's presence.

"Nor did He enter heaven to offer Himself again and again, the way the high priest enters the Most Holy Place every year with blood that is not his own. Then Christ would have had to suffer many times since the creation of the world. But now He has appeared once for all at the end of the ages to do away with sin by the sacrifice of Himself" (Hebrews 9:23-26).

A Quiet View of the Graveyard

I already mentioned that my small community college overlooked a large cemetery. The view sparked some strange comments from time to time. For instance, we were pretty sure where the college administration had dug up some of the teachers. But the location was a good reminder too. Death is one experience we often push aside with little thought. But Christianity offers an incredible courtesy: It reminds us, even through the prominence of blood, that life here is not permanent.

"Just as man is destined to die once, and after that to face judgment, so Christ was sacrificed once to take away the sins of many people; and He will appear a second time, not to bear sin, but to bring salvation to those who are waiting for Him" (Hebrews 9:27-28).

There is an Ultimate Tomorrow which, apart from Jesus, is a terrifying prospect. Without Him, we can anticipate nothing but certain judgment and outer darkness. Through Him, we can rise up from the shadows without fear of judgment, with a clean conscience, and expecting unimaginable joy.

Prodigal's world changed abruptly. He had stood, engulfed in the Sonshine, reflecting on the wonderful-yet-desolating things that had been revealed. But then, without warning, they had all vanished and he was standing at the edge of the highway at twilight. The Son, low on the western horizon, blood red, had returned to its normal dimensions. In fact, everything was as it had been before his encounter with the Sonshine, except . . .

Except . . . now, rather than facing east, away from the Son, Prodigal had turned west, toward it. Even so, he would have figured the encounter to have been some psychic hallucination had it not been for the small leather-bound Book, still clutched in his hand.

Then he remembered his backpack. He had stripped off that encumbrance when he ran toward the Son. He glanced toward the guard rail beside the road. The pack was gone.

Prodigal stood, in the early evening shadows, perplexed, mentally retracing his exhilarating encounter with the Son which now seemed so distant, so other-worldly. And he wondered, *Had anything really changed?*

9

Our dark times would have remained a perplexing mystery had it not been for the experience of the Son. But the time came when even He endured darkness, when there was . . .

Sonshine in Shadow Valley

Often, as I was growing up, people pointed to John as an example to follow. We had always been close; we played together constantly.

One Sunday morning I walked over to John's to see if he could play. His dad was out in the workshop, in his work clothes, tinkering with some project.

"Can John come out and play?" I asked, over the drone of his jigsaw.

John's father scowled at me then said, condescendingly, *"Johnny's* at church."

I felt foolish for having asked. It didn't occur to me at the time that it was a bit hypocritical of Johnny's father to chide me about church attendance as he stood, so to speak, up to his armpits in sawdust.

It wasn't long before I started going to church with John. We were in the same Sunday School class, which was fun. But Johnny went to church camp and I didn't. The Sunday following camp, the pastor's wife had an announcement to make during the opening exercises of the Junior Department

Sunday School we attended.

"Johnny asked Jesus into his heart at camp this week," she beamed.

I was envious. It sounded neat.

I later wondered why she hadn't explained what that meant. Or how you got Jesus into your heart. Or why no one would tell me. Or had all that happened and I just forgot?

As we got older, I started getting into trouble at school. At home, the family relationships were getting strained. But not at Johnny's house. They had it all together. Why couldn't I be more like John? And our family more like his?

Now I have some questions:

Why is it that, in spite of my rebellion, I kept going to church and ultimately turned to God, but John dumped his Christianity?

And why, years later, had my marriage lasted, while his disintegrated after less than a year?

And how are things between John and Jesus now? Did he receive the Friendly Invasion of the Son-Word for keeps? Or was his faith a hoax?

The experiences John and I had raised a bigger question: *Once we make a commitment to Jesus, once we accept the Friendly Invasion of the Son-Word, how can we keep that commitment?*

And the related question: *Why do some make it while others do not?*

These questions are answered with two clear principles (Hebrews 10). *Principle # 1:* A follower of the Son *can* keep his commitment; it is possible (10:1-18). *Principle # 2:* A follower of the Son *must* keep his commitment; it is mandatory (10:19-39).

The old-system/new-system contrast, developed

in chapter 9, is explained in Hebrews 10:1-18. Through the blood of Jesus, God has introduced a new covenant, the Son-Word System. Through faith in Jesus, and with appreciation for His death in our place, we can begin life again—with a clean conscience.

The writer takes us deeper (Hebrews 10): "The Law is only a shadow of the good things that are coming—not the realities themselves. For this reason it can never, by the same sacrfices repeated endlessly year after year, make perfect those who draw near to worship" (10:1).

These are the key words: *the same sacrifices, repeated endlessly, year after year.* The priests who offered all those bloody sacrifices and the people for whom they were offered should have seen the point. If the same sacrifice has to be made over and over, something must be missing.

If those repeated sacrifices could have done the job, would they not have stopped being offered? For the worshipers would have been cleansed once for all, and would no longer have felt guilty for their sins.

"But those sacrifices are an annual reminder of sins, because it is impossible for the blood of bulls and goats to take away sins" (10:2—4).

If we were still offering repetitive, gory death-sacrifices, killing animals to demonstrate our repentant hearts, our religious commitments might probably soon flicker and die, as many of theirs did. But God planned more.

The Bible Tells Me So

Had Jesus not invaded this planet, had He not been born, had He not become a once-for-all sacrifice, we might wonder if God expected us to shift for ourselves spiritually—in which case we *would* make religious commitments we couldn't keep.

Here's fascinating insight into Jesus' attitude toward His strange mission to invade the planet in friendliness and love: "When Christ came into the world, He said: 'Sacrifice and offering You [God] did not desire, but a body You prepared for Me; with burnt offerings and sin offerings You were not pleased' " (10:5-6).

Jesus' response to God's plan is incredible. "Here I am—it is written about Me in the scroll—I have come to do Your will, O God" (10:7).

It's as if Jesus is saying: "I have seen how they grab a defenseless woolly lamb. I have seen how they cut it apart. I have seen the blood. I know that kind of sacrifice is not adequate. If that's all there is, they will be killing lambs forever, but will not have clear consciences, nor will they be free from guilt. They will make religious commitments, maybe, but often they will be unable to keep them. I will become a sacrifice. My body will be broken and My blood splattered."

It is this sacrifice by Jesus that the New Covenant, the Son-Word System, is built on. It is infinitely better, because God has become His own sacrifice. Hebrews 10:8-10 explains it:

"First, He [Jesus] said, 'Sacrifices and offerings, burnt offerings, and sin offerings You [God] did not desire, nor were You pleased with them' (although the Law required them to be made). Then He said, 'Here I am, I have come to do Your will.' He sets aside the first to establish the second. And by that will [God's], we have been made holy through the sacrifice of the body of Jesus Christ once for all."

Been Made and Being Made

Now there are five words to wonder about: "We have been made holy." Who? When? How? Holy?

The point is, sincere faith in Jesus—mine, yours, John's, anybody's—sparks a curious transaction.

"God made Him who had no sin to be sin for us, so that in Him we might become the righteousness of God" (2 Corinthians 5:21).

When we accept the Friendly Invasion of the Son-Word, God puts our badness on Jesus and His goodness on us. As imperfect as we still are, He labels believers as "holy." How is it that our guilt could be crated and shipped out?

"Day after day every priest stands and performs his religious duties; again and again he offers the same sacrifices, which can never take away sins. But when this Priest [Jesus] had offered for all time one sacrifice for sins, He sat down at the right hand of God. Since that time He waits for His enemies to be made His footstool, because by one sacrifice He has made perfect forever those who are being made holy" (10:11-14. Now there's something else to wonder about: Who "are being made holy"?

The point is that in Jesus, God has labeled Christians holy, but then expects us—with His help—to live up to the label. That is the Son-Word System, the New Covenant.

"The Holy Spirit also testifies to us about this. First He says, 'This is the covenant I will make with them after that time, says the Lord. I will put My laws in their hearts, and I will write them on their minds.' Then he adds: 'Their sins and lawless acts I will remember no more.' And where these have been forgiven, there is no longer any sacrifice for sin" (Hebrews 10:15-18).

That's *Principle #1:* A follower of the Son *can* keep his commitment; it is possible. God has labeled us holy and is helping us to live up to that label. We stand on a foundation of full forgiveness, a clean conscience.

There Has to Be a Perfect Word

Several years ago, after being out of the Southern California area for some time, I returned for a visit. John was home from Northern California visiting his parents the same time I was there visiting mine. John and I talked, for perhaps five minutes, standing in his parents' front yard at dusk.

It was an awkward conversation, like two strangers trying to find a hunk of common ground to construct a conversation on. I thought, *There just has to be a right word, an appropriate comment.*

I wanted John to understand that I still considered him a friend, that I cared about his broken marriage. But I wanted him to understand too that there was a way back into the Sonshine, that he could once again be close to God.

I imagine there was a sensitive and tactful way to say all that, without John feeling like a target of a rampaging Jesus freak. But I couldn't pull it off. And I haven't seen John since. I still wonder, *How are things between him and Jesus? Is there someone close to John who is also close to Jesus, someone to point the way back? What was going on in John's mind the day he turned his back on Jesus and discarded his discipleship?*

I'm convinced of *Principle #1:* A follower of the

Son *can* keep his commitment; it is possible. But the writer has also made me aware of the seriousness of *Principle #2:* A follower of the Son *must* keep his commitment: It is mandatory.

This second principle includes an encouragement, a warning, a reminder, and a promise.

Isosceles Never Had It So Good

The *encouragement* is threefold, the ol' faith-hope-and-love triangle. This encouragement triangle sits on a firm foundation—a restatement of *Principle #1:*

"Therefore, brothers, since we have confidence to enter the Most Holy Place by the blood of Jesus, by a new and living way opened for us through the curtain, that is, His body, and since we have a great Priest over the house of God ..." (Hebrews 10:19-21).

In other words, because God has made it possible to keep our commitment to Him; because He has forgiven us; because He has cleaned up our consciences, taking away our moral dirt; because of all this, we *must* keep our commitment. Keeping the commitment involves *faith*:

"Let us draw near to God with a sincere heart in full assurance of faith, having our hearts sprinkled to cleanse us from a guilty conscience and having our bodies washed with pure water" (Hebrews 10:22).

Jesus, God's One Final Blazing Word, has given us a huge advantage: Through His death He has given us a direct line to God. To return to the tabernacle/tent-in-the-wilderness illustration, rather than waiting for a priest to offer a sacrifice for us,

Christ has gone into the Most Holy Place as our Representative. So we can "draw near to God." We can talk over our hassles, discuss our temptations, speak with Him about our doubts. We do so knowing we have His full attention and that He regards us as morally pure as His own Son. It's part of the Son-Word agreement.

We *must* keep our commitment to the Son. But He has made it easier to do so; He has given us direct communication with His Father.

Keeping our commitment to the Son also involves the encouragement of an unbobbing *hope*, which points toward the future and all God has planned for us. We struggle with our own cruddy moral weakness, *now*. We may be plagued with doubts, question what God is trying to accomplish, in view of pain, starvation, war, inhumanity, broken relationships, and hassles with parents: *Now* we scuffle with doubt.

But that's just it: The way God has it planned, the conflicts are *all* now. The second side of His encouragement triangle is *hope*. God has the future worked out, an elaborate blueprint of joy, certain to be constructed. *Faithful* means He will deliver, it will happen. Our side of the hope coin is stamped, "Hang in there; it's worth the effort."

The third element of this encouragement triangle is *love*, a big part of keeping our commitment to the Son.

"Let us consider how we may spur one another on toward love and good deeds. Let us not give up meeting together, as some are in the habit of doing, but let us encourage one another—and all the more as you see the Day approaching" (Hebrews 10:24-25).

I sit here reflecting on my friends who have

cashed in their Christianity. John, who let things slip, probably as a gradual process of neglect. Cindy, who changed boyfriends and junked the church. Mike, who couldn't make the break with old habits and the downward pull of "wrong friends." Jeff, who, it would seem, had merely conned everyone into thinking he had left his "old ways." And others.

I just can't help wondering, *How many of these "Christians" would have remained true to their commitment to follow the Son if only love—this one part of the triangle—were working for them?*

Even when our temptations or doubts or struggles are strongest, we can make it if only someone's there who cares, someone who, in love, holds us up. That's a big part of what the church is all about. It is to be a home of care and concern, a place where we are urged to do good.

I note that Christians often bring out the worst in one another. We make it hard for another Christian to forgive his parents because we are so quick to say, "Boy, you really do have it bad!"

We may make it tough for a handicapped kid to cope because we insensitively toss ridicule or pity his way. We make it a humongous task for each other to achieve any level of moral purity.

We must keep our commitments to the Son. Part of the commitment to Him is commitment to one another, to "spur one another on toward love and good deeds."

A Little More than Friendly Persuasion

Perhaps we are so careless about our commitments to the Son and to one another *because* God *has* made it possible to keep those commitments. After all, if God's love motivated His Son to be the bloody Sacrifice to clean our conscience and lift our guilt, we can relax. If He peers at us from heaven and labels us "holy," knowing we aren't, it seems that He must have low standards—a lenient disposition.

Perhaps we once read, "Shall we go on sinning so that grace may increase? By no means!" (Romans 6:1-2). All the God-love talk is just too much. When it comes to life, we take the first choices; God is welcome to the leftovers.

We've earned the warning: "If we deliberately keep on sinning after we have received the knowledge of the truth, no sacrifice for sins is left, but only a fearful expectation of judgment and of raging fire that will consume the enemies of God" (Hebrews 10:26-27).

It's true: God gives new life on the basis of faith-not-works. The Friendly Invasion of the Son-Word is really a friendly invasion. Jesus comes in love, and He comes to stay. But the question persists: *How do we know our invitation to Him was sincere, our faith real?*

What can we point to that will make us feel secure? That we walked an aisle, or mumbled, "Jesus, come in"? The evidence the Bible invites us to point to is a changed life. We moved out of the Wilderness of Death. We put our personal mutiny behind.

The warning continues: "Anyone who rejected the Law of Moses died without mercy on the testimony of two or three witnesses. How much more severely do you think a man deserves to be punished who has trampled the Son of God under foot, who has treated as an unholy thing the blood of the covenant that sanctified him, and who has insulted the Spirit of grace? For we know Him who said, 'It is Mine to avenge; I will repay,' and again, 'The Lord will judge His people.' It is a dreadful thing to fall into the hands of the living God" (Hebrews 10:28-31).

Sonshine also scorches.

The Farther You Fall, the More It Hurts

Everyone was thrilled by Randy's conversion. The change was drastic. No more drugs, drinking, or stealing. All three had been deeply engrained habits. It was surprising Randy fared so well as a Christian. His family problems had been intense and he was now homeless. That's when a Christian family opened their doors and made him a part of them. It wasn't long before they discovered that Randy was lying to them, and that the sterling saint wasn't so sterling.

For many of us, Randy became an illustration of the simple principle: *The farther you fall, the more it hurts.* And the more it hurts the one who fell, the more it hurts everyone close to him.

The Book of Hebrews was originally written to Christian Jews who were seriously considering tossing out Christianity and hiking back into the Old Covenant. The writer warns that to do so would incur devastating judgment. And the reminder is added, the farther you fall, the more it hurts.

"Remember those earlier days after you had received the Light, when you stood your ground in a great contest in the face of suffering. Sometimes you were publicly exposed to insult and persecution; at other times you stood side by side with those who were so treated. You sympathized with those in prison and joyfully accepted the confiscation of your property, because you knew that you yourselves had better and lasting possessions" (Hebrews 10:32-34).

It occurs to me, if *these* people needed this horrible warning, what would God have to say to us?

A Promise More than a Possibility

I think of John and Randy, and I wonder: *Once we make a commitment to Jesus, can we keep it?*

God's writer answers forcefully with two principles: *Principle #1:* A follower of the Son *can* keep his commitment; it is possible (10:1-18). God's One Final Blazing Word has made the way. *Principle #2:* A follower of the Son *must* keep his commitment; it is mandatory (10:19-39). When these commitments to the Son are shattered, they always break into the shape of a question mark: *Is that person truly a follower of the Son?*

"So do not throw away your confidence; it will be richly rewarded. You need to persevere so that when you have done the will of God, you will receive what He has promised.

"For in just a very little while, 'He who is coming will come and will not delay. But My righteous one will live by faith. And if he shrinks back, I will not be pleased with him' " (Hebrews 10:35-38).

And a final encouraging word:

"But we are not of those who shrink back and are destroyed, but of those who believe and are saved" (Hebrews 10:39).

It is this belief that starts the Friendly Invasion.

"Is it possible," Prodigal reflected aloud, "that I have been wrong about my encounter with the Son?"

Reflexively, his grip tightened on the small Book. He gazed across the open land, down the long asphalt ribbon, to the horizon. Then he perceived for the first time that the Son now appeared to be setting. It was less bright than it had been only moments earlier. His pulse quickened. He realized there had to have been a change in him. He had never before feared darkness. Now he found its reality cold, terrifying.

He began walking westward, toward the setting Son, but soon turned his collar up against the chill and quickened his pace. Moments later he was sprinting, trying to outrun the deepening darkness.

That's when he saw Him, standing quietly in the shadows. Even before he could distinguish any definite characteristics, he knew it was Traveler, the brother-like Visitor he had encountered earlier.

Traveler read the panic in Prodigal's gray face and spoke one rapid sentence:

"Use the Book."

Prodigal looked down at this hand, stared blankly at the Book, and stammered, "But the darkness? . . ."

Prodigal looked again at the Book and cracked it open. Instantaneously, he was surrounded by a strange luminescent glow.

10

Our perplexing times are nagging reminders that things aren't right on the Son's Planet. As much as we are prone to settle here, through faith we should look up to find . . .

Home at Son City

I don't know why courthouses seem to be such cold, impersonal buildings. Perhaps that's by design. But on December 18, 1976, we entered one of those large, frigidly impersonal stone buildings for a legal session that was to be the final kink in the red-tape tangle of our son's adoption. If this proceeding went as we hoped, we would be free to adopt our foster son, Schaun. If not, he would be returned to an environment of severe neglect.

That morning my silent anger peaked. Anger at a system that had allowed a young life to remain in an insecure limbo, a ward of the court, for more than three years. A child of four is too old for his permanent home to be a needlessly unsettled question.

The night before we had been uptight, knowing the final resolution was far from clear-cut. The social worker was skeptical. After all, this was something of a test case under a new law. Besides, the judge who was to preside had a reputation for side-stepping difficult decisions, holding them "under advisement" for months, even years.

That morning we drove to the attorney's office, then walked together down broad sidewalks, up stone steps to the courthouse, an imposing gray building. Inside, the poorly lit halls stretched out in dull walls and drab flooring, designed to look like cut marble. I guess it was tile, though I wouldn't be surprised if it were just some swirly designs on linoleum.

The "meeting" was to be upstairs, so we climbed the steep steps, hanging on to a railing that felt like a beam of ice. Upstairs, we settled in a small room. It too was cold and impersonal, lined with shelves of law books. I sat on a gray metal folding chair in front of a window air conditioner that invited in the winter draft through poorly sealed sides.

This was the moment toward which so many of our prayers had been directed for a year and a half. This morning's meeting was the ultimate ingredient to be tossed into the crucible of our faith—the final exam in some strange class on God's will. People had carelessly assured us, "Of course, it'll all work out!" But the agony was knowing that God was not obligated to work *any* of it out. He would remain good and loving even if He chose to answer no to our year-and-a-half prayer: "Lord, let us adopt Schaun."

It is through difficult times, not breezy experiences, that our faith is tested, refined. And so, to Jewish Christians undergoing persecution from Rome and ridicule from their fellow Jews, the letter we call *Hebrews* came as an encouragement to live by faith. Faith comes to us in the same way. It's when our hard times meet with our beliefs that other people can observe us responding in a unique and compelling way.

The writer of Hebrews 10 spells it out:

"In just a very little while, 'He who is coming will come and will not delay. But my righteous one will live by faith. And if he shrinks back, I will not be pleased with him' " (10:37-38).

But what is faith?

How is it to be expressed?

Is it fair of God to expect us to believe when confronted with opposition or uncertainty?

The answer to these questions is found in the 11th chapter of Hebrews. In that chapter, a few introductory words on faith are followed by a number of Old Testament examples. Each example relates to that first verse:

"Now faith is being sure of what we hope for and certain of what we do not see. This is what the ancients were commended for" (Hebrews 11:1-2).

Faith is tied to the future ("what we hope for"). There is a mutiny on the Son's Planet. The whole system seems out of kilter now. Conditions are abnormal. We will not be settled until we are home at Son City. But God is going to change that mutiny . . . in the future.

"For in just a very little while, 'He who is coming will come and will not delay' " (Hebrews 10:37). Faith is rooted in a confidence, a hope, that there will be a second Invasion of the Son. The mutiny will be crushed in judgment. Everything that now brings sorrow will be brought into line with the Son's purposes.

Faith is tied to the invisible ("what we do not see"). The New Testament presents *faith* and *sight* in contrast to each other. "We live by faith, not by sight" (2 Corinthians 5:7). If we have the outcome of our hassles all wrapped up, skillfully packaged, with no questions or no doubts, would we need faith? Not really.

It is in the dark times, when we cannot see the outcome, that faith glows.

Seen from Unseen

What better way to illustrate the concept of faith than pointing to Creation? Since we weren't around at the beginning-point of Creation, and since we can never scientifically repeat it and observe it, any assumption of how it all started must come by faith.

"By faith we understand that the universe was formed at God's command, so that what is seen was not made out of what was visible" (Hebrews 11:3).

Without faith, page 1 of the Bible can't be figured out. And without faith, the message of Hebrews won't help us. Of Israel it was said, "The message they heard was of no value to them, because those who heard did not combine it with faith" (Hebrews 4:2). The same is true today. Creation stands as an allegory of faith. We can't "prove" God right, nor can we "prove" Him wrong.

In the same way, we encounter dark perplexing times—a good friend critically ill, a marriage breaking up, a temptation we can't handle. We have no idea why God permits such difficult circumstances—there is that "invisible" element. It is in such circumstances that God challenges us to express faith.

In hard times, it's tempting to select a rosy outcome and then pin our faith on that. After all, if it's what we want, what we think is best, for sure, God will give us just what we ask for or something better.

The prospects might be bleak—suffering, death, financial hassles, rejection by our peers. Surely, we tell ourselves, if we just have *enough faith*, God will perform the stunt and everything will be OK.

The problem is, regardless of sincere prayer, cancer patients still die, wars are still waged, famines still come, children still suffer, relationships are still broken. That does not necessarily mean that the faith was inadequate, or misplaced.

Faith would be a simple matter if only God would promise to give us exactly what we think we need. Then there would be no questions. No dark times. No unseen elements. Prayer would become a contest in creative hoping in which we would plug in a bit of "faith" and *zap* . . . the answer!

But it's precisely when we are least sure of the outcome, when we know things could bomb out, that faith has the greatest chance to grow. The question is: Can we trust God if our friend does die? If you're never accepted by the group you'd like to join, will you still keep your commitment to the Son? Will you keep your faith if you lose your job, your health, your boyfriend or girlfriend? Or if God does not drastically change your looks, your I.Q., or your personality?

Is your faith nailed to a nice income? Or to the powerful Person who just may not always agree with you?

He Isn't a Tame Lion

In C.S. Lewis' *Chronicles of Narnia*, the land of Narnia, a rightful possession of Aslan the noble lion, is often controlled by people who hate the lion and his ways. The White Witch rules the land and makes it "always winter and never Christmas." The Telmarines conquer the tiny Narnian kingdom and try to blot out the stories of this strange beast.

All the time the lion is away, the question recurs, "Is there a great lion at all? Is he really in charge? Is this the way he would run things?"

Yet, even when the lion returns and is unmistakably in control, his followers constantly remind one another, *"He is not a tame lion!"*

In the same way, God is not predictable. We can never assume that our best ideas should be His plan. Faith means that we give up our efforts at taming God, and stop insisting that He follow our course of action.

And how might we try to tame God? With our faith, our prayers, maybe even with an unspoken threat that we'll quit believing in Him if He withholds our requests.

Hebrews-11-style faith sees circumstances in the bigger framework of the Son's plan.

There is a mutiny on the Son's Planet.

It will change. God is the Lord of time.

For the present, He has allowed a lot of freedom for things to "malfunction."

A willingness to go with that flow is what faith is all about. It's spelled out in Hebrews 11 for any who would question, "How does the idea work out in practical experience?"

Three before the Fathers

Trusting God in the dark is not a new concept. Even from the beginning, before the nation of

Israel, there were some people who were sure of what they hoped for and certain of what they did not see.

Better sacrifice than Cain ...

"By faith Abel offered God a better sacrifice than Cain did. By faith he was commended as a righteous man, when God spoke well of his offerings. And by faith he still speaks, even though he is dead" (Hebrews 11:4).

Abel did not have the benefit of a huge Bible to spell out all his directions for living. He acted on what he knew God wanted and was praised for his faith.

Check out the story of these heirs of Adam and Eve, in Genesis 4:1-15.

Airborne by faith ...

"By faith Enoch was taken from this life, so that he did not experience death; he could not be found, because God had taken him away. For before he was taken, he was commended as one who pleased God. And without faith it is impossible to please God, because anyone who comes to Him must believe that He exists and that He rewards those who earnestly seek Him" (Hebrews 11:5-6).

Can you imagine what it was like, looking for Enoch? "Well, he was here just a minute ago." Not that Enoch is an example of a classy way to escape death (God isn't tame or ordinary). Enoch is a sterling example of faith—a rare person who kept living a consistent life after his peers had junked the idea of living right. Enoch's faith pleased God. God enjoyed having him around ... enjoyed it a lot!

Enoch's short story is found in Genesis 5:21-24.

Hark an ark!

"By faith Noah, when warned about things not yet seen, in holy fear built an ark to save his family.

By his faith he condemned the world and became heir of the righteousness that comes by faith" (Hebrews 11:7).

"Noah," the routine goes, "build Me a boat!"

"A huh? What's a . . . a . . . a boat?"

"It's going to rain, Noah," the scenario continues.

"Rain? What's rain?"

You couldn't really say the story is funny. Far from it. Yet, it certainly is ironic. It had not yet rained on earth. And who would need a boat on dry land.

No one likes it when a weatherman gives a pessimistic report. But Noah was worse than that. He preached an unpopular message for 120 years and still got no takers except his family. By faith Noah acted on a clear word from God, even though it meant standing alone.

Pick up the story in Genesis 6; don't stop at 7.

Don't Know Where I'm Goin' but Glad to Go

Then there are the Founding Fathers of the nation of Israel . . .

Stranger in a foreign country . . .

"By faith Abraham, when called to go to a place he would later receive as his inheritance, obeyed and went, even though he did not know where he was going. By faith he made his home in the promised land like a stranger in a foreign country; he lived in tents, as did Isaac and Jacob, who were heirs with him of the same promise. For he was looking forward to the city with foundations, whose Architect and Builder is God" (Hebrews 11:8-10).

Apparently Abraham knew God had something better for him than Canaan Land, even though it was flowing with milk and honey. By faith in God, Abraham was willing to live out his life as one long camping trip.

Genesis 12 will get you going on Abraham's story.

Stars and sand forever . . .

"By faith Abraham, even though he was past age—and Sarah herself was barren—was enabled to become a father because he considered Him faithful who had made the promise. And so from this one man, and he as good as dead, came descendants as numerous as the stars in the sky and as countless as the sand on the seashore" (Hebrews 11:11-12).

By faith this couple in their 90s first believed that they were to have a child. A laughable prospect to Sarah. And, likewise by faith, the promise was fulfilled—after Abraham's 100th birthday. So it was that these spunky senior citizens became parents and started a big family tree.

The whole story is Genesis nonstop, from chapters 12 to 18, and beyond.

More than Canaan, not less than heaven . . .

"All these people were still living by faith when they died. They did not receive the things promised; they only saw them and welcomed them from a distance. And they admitted that they were aliens and strangers on earth. People who say such things show that they are looking for a country of their own. If they had been thinking of the country they had left, they would have had opportunity to return. Instead, they were longing for a better country—a heavenly one. Therefore God is not ashamed to be called their God, for He has prepared a city for them" (Hebrews 11:13-16).

There is just something about faith that hangs on when things are discouraging and God seems silent. This is the point at which faith is graphically demonstrated—when it is tied to the future and to the invisible. The values that are expressed in this style of faith come from Son City, the Ultimate Home.

Sacrifice altered ...

"By faith Abraham, when God tested him, offered Isaac as a sacrifice. He who had received the promises was about to sacrifice his one and only son, even though God had said to him, 'It is through Isaac that your offspring will be reckoned.' Abraham reasoned that God could raise the dead and, figuratively speaking, he did receive Isaac back from death" (Hebrews 11:17-19).

This example is interesting because not only was Abraham's faith resting on God's Word, but there was a seeming contradiction. Because of his faith, Abraham assumed it was God's job to somehow straighten out the conflicting messages: (a) the promises will come through Isaac; (b) kill him.

Not that the faith wasn't costly. Abraham cared for Isaac, it's clear. Yet this vivid faith-display stands for us both as a frightening example of costly faith, and as a comforting example of God's sensitive and loving response.

Read about it in Genesis 22; you owe it to yourself.

Three generations and onward ...

"By faith Isaac blessed Jacob and Esau in regard to their future. By faith Jacob, when he was dying, blessed each of Joseph's sons, and worshiped as he leaned on the top of his staff. By faith Joseph, when his end was near, spoke about the exodus of the Israelites from Egypt and gave instructions about his bones" (Hebrews 11:20-22).

These were people who expected God to keep His promise, regardless of His timing. People who felt a part of some ongoing plan God was revealing. People who looked back on adversities and failures and yet dared to believe that God would keep His Word anyhow. Here's more about such people.

High Hopes in a Wet Wicker Basket

By now it should be clear to any thoroughbred Jew that the principle of faith is central to their noble heritage. But for any who might still be wondering, the writer points to the nation's superhero, Moses.

Baby with promise . . .

"By faith Moses' parents hid him for three months after he was born, because they saw he was no ordinary child, and they were not afraid of the king's edict" (Hebrews 11:23).

Even Moses' folks showed faith in ignoring the Pharaoh's command that all Hebrew newborns were to be murdered. Faith gave courage. And it still does.

Check Exodus 1—2 for more insight.

Don't call me "Egyptian" . . .

"By faith Moses, when he had grown up, refused to be known as the son of Pharaoh's daughter. He chose to be mistreated along with the people of God rather than to enjoy the pleasures of sin for a short time. He regarded disgrace for the sake of Christ as of greater value than the treasures of Egypt, because he was looking ahead to his reward" (Hebrews 11:24-26).

Given the choice of comfort or conflict, Moses chose conflict. Chalk it up to his faith. Faith colored his value system and made it more accurate, really, by introducing the element of eternity. When judged by time only, comfort and pleasure most always win. But introduce a cosmic dimension, an eternal perspective, and the order of importance shifts. It did for Moses.

See what can't be seen . . .

"By faith he left Egypt, not fearing the king's anger; he persevered because he saw Him who is invisible. By faith he kept the Passover and the sprinkling of blood, so that the destroyer of the firstborn would not touch the firstborn of Israel" (Hebrews 11:27-28).

Here's a guy who grew up to copy his parents. As they had not feared the king's edict, preserving *his* life, he did not fear the king's anger and was able to be the nation's deliverer. It happened by faith. And how could Moses hang in there? By seeing Him who is invisible. And the theme returns: *faith!*

Exodus 5—12 gives the unusual background details.

How dry the land . . .

"By faith the people passed through the Red Sea as on dry land; but when the Egyptians tried to do so, they were drowned" (Hebrews 11:29).

And where is faith here? When you're leading a whole nation of people and are being chased by warlike Egyptians and you come to the Red Sea with nowhere to go but wet, faith swings into operation. God gave the directions, Moses followed them, even under jeering stress from his perturbed peers.

More words on the wet and the dry: Exodus 13—14.

On across the Jordan . . .

"By faith the walls of Jericho fell, after the people had marched around them for seven days. By faith the prostitute Rahab, because she welcomed the spies, was not killed with those who were disobedient" (Hebrews 11:30-31).

About 40 years after the Red Sea incident, and after an interruption of unbelief, another generation of Jews showed that the faith principle was still operating. Faithlessness had sidetracked the big favors from God and had brought judgment. But when faith returned, so did some remarkable displays of God's power. It isn't every day that walled cities collapse with a shout, all because of faith. That is, unless you count the walled cities we experience: feelings of insecurity, past failures, broken relationships. In that sense, God is still breaking down "walled cities," doing the impossible, joyfully.

The first six chapters of Joshua give the story of Jericho, Rahab, and Israel. For the story of today's faith-gifts, talk to the followers of the Son. Christians around the world are finding that by faith they can be sure of what they hope for and certain of what they do not see. And even when God seems to withhold the good things, the big favors, even then (maybe especially then) they can hold on. Because really, things here are temporary. God has promised to untangle all our confused questions when we get home to Son City.

New Year's Son

Finally, it happened, after a year and a half of concerned prayer, Schaun was free to be adopted. That morning was cold. The lighted sign on the First National Bank that usually spelled out advertising slogans interspersed with the time and temperature, instead ran an animation of two cars skidding on ice and sliding into a collision, followed by the temperature—around zero.

Once again we walked broad concrete sidewalks and climbed stone steps. Again we entered the county courthouse, still cold and impersonal. But that morning Schaun became our son, our heir-by-law.

No way can I re-create on paper the trauma those 18 months of uncertainty brought. But neither can I adequately express the joy of trusting a God who is big enough to bring order out of chaos—even in those many experiences when the chaos seemed as if it were going to be lifelong.

There is a mutiny on the Son's Planet. It affects every area of life. But that mutiny is temporary; it will change. The truly remarkable thing is this: We can trust God's One Final Blazing Word until we are home in Son City.

"And what more shall I say? I do not have time to tell about Gideon, Barak, Samson, Jephthah, David, Samuel, and the prophets, who through faith conquered kingdoms, administered justice, and gained what was promised; who shut the mouths of lions, quenched the fury of flames, and escaped the edge of the sword; whose weakness was turned to strength; and who became powerful in battle and routed foreign armies. Women received back their dead, raised to life again.

"Others were tortured and refused to be released, so that they might gain a better resurrection. Some faced jeers and flogging, while still others were chained and put in prison. They were stoned; they were sawed in two, they were put to death by the sword. They went about in sheepskins and goatskins, destitute, persecuted, and mistreated—the world was not worthy of them. They wandered in deserts and mountains, and in caves and holes in the ground.

"These were all commended for their faith, yet none of them received what had been promised. God had planned something better for us so that only together with us would they be made perfect" (Hebrews 11:32-40).

Prodigal had been so intrigued by the Book that he had not noticed when Traveler slipped away into the shadows. Instead, he sat down in the middle of the deserted highway to read.

"It is often in the darkness that the most enlightening concepts are learned," he read. "But a follower of the Son cannot settle in the darkness as if at home, for his ultimate home is the blazing core of the Son itself."

But the concept that arrested his attention was the simple phrase, "There is darkness of circumstance and there is darkness of character. One is part of every man's life, the other must never be."

Intrigued that something as common as a Book could give light, Prodigal read for hours, sitting cross-legged on the highway, his body huddled over the crisp, glowing pages.

Light. He turned the word in his mind at length. *Light and warmth.* His mind was transfixed . . . not as one in a hypnotic stupor; more like one in awe of some new and unexpected concept.

And, settled in the darkness, he continued to read.

146

11

Whether we seem close to God or distant,
whether we feel "religious" or rotten, whether
we know it or not, what we all need is . . .

Warmth from the Father of the Son

David was listless, sitting on the edge of the bed, lost in thought. Beside him was a letter, the envelope torn across its face. It had been opened in haste and anticipation. Now it was tossed aside in discouragement.

When he was younger he had determined that he would someday become a fighter pilot. But unlike other kids with glamorous vocational objectives, David went after it with zeal, even into his teen years. He did not "grow out of it" as his parents had assumed he would. Instead, his interest intensified. He bought dozens of books on flying and aerodynamics and any remotely related topic.

Throughout his high school years, David had noticed problems with his eyes and finally had to get glasses. When the lenses did not completely correct his vision, he knew his long-standing plans would have to be put aside. To be sure, he enlisted in the Air Force, but discovered that the problem was worse than he had thought. Not only would he be ineligible for pilot's training, he could not get in the service at all.

David's discouragement was intensified by other people's lack of understanding. When he would share his frustration and disappointment with friends, they would respond by asking, "What on earth would make you want to join the service anyway?" At first, he would try to explain, but soon gave up. No one understood or seemed to care.

For years, David's parents had wrestled with marital problems. Now, even though those problems had improved considerably, David felt their full force, perhaps for the first time. With his career frustrations, his resistance was low. But once again, he had trouble finding anyone who would listen or could understand. After all, the problems *had* improved.

Over the few years that followed, David applied to a few companies associated with different facets of the commercial aviation industry. Due to his lack of training, he was unable to even get an interview for a position. When he finally found a company that expressed slight interest, he pinned his hopes on that one company. This letter was the one he had been expecting, a reply to his formal application. Not that he anticipated a job offer or official word. But, he had hoped, they would at least suggest he come in for an interview.

He had torn open the envelope enthusiastically and quickly scanned the letter. Rather than the promising words he had expected, the letter (written by a secretary) had said, "No openings."

David knew that other people received discouraging letters all the time. It wasn't true that the world was against him. But with his backlog of discouragement and depression, the letter was just too much to take. This job had not been his first choice. Far from it. Now even his alternate plans were being frustrated.

Frustrations, disappointments, pain—these things easily extinguish the sizzling joy of our relationship with Jesus, God's One Final Blazing Word. We receive the Friendly Invasion of the Son-Word and fully expect our experiences to be different. After all, if God is on our side and if He controls everything, it is only natural to expect special treatment. Christian marriages should be hassle-free, we think. Children of the Son should not have to work hard for good grades. Believers should never get the flu. Pious folks should never have acne problems. The devout should get the best jobs.

And more than that: Tornadoes should skip over the homes of Bible-believers, taking nothing more than a barn and a silo. Earthquakes should not shake people whose lives are built on the Rock. Car accidents should be miraculously avoided when Christians are at the wheel, or in the passenger's seat, or anywhere in the vicinity.

Unfortunately, it doesn't work that way. There is a mutiny on the Son's Planet. It affects us all. We may put our own personal mutiny aside, we may live life in the Cosmic Dimension, but it doesn't guarantee we'll miss the hassles, the discouragements, the pain that goes with an abnormal world awaiting the Second Invasion of the Son.

Until the Return of Jesus, when He will set everything straight, we all need warmth from the Father of the Son. We need the soothing warmth of encouragement, the joy of knowing we belong to Him and He cares. But we also need the scorching heat of His discipline, the reminder that His Word must be taken seriously. Our lives must change. In

Hebrews, chapter 12, we're exposed to the warmth of the Father, reminding us of His encouragement (we too are His sons and daughters) and warns us of His discipline (He cares enough to correct us).

Eyes Fixed, Heart Strong

It all goes back to faith. In Hebrews 11 faith is pictured as the vital element in conquering kingdoms, administering justice, and obtaining promises. Because of faith, some righteous people did not become lions' feed, were not charred in fiery furnaces, were not punctured by swords. Faith made weak people strong—they did incredible things in battle, won some precarious wars. Because of faith, some resurrections took place, breaking up a few funeral processions. Remarkable (Hebrews 11:32-35).

And yet, not everyone had such good fortune. Other people, with the same kind of faith, were laughed at, tortured, beaten, imprisoned. Some were stoned, sawed in two, or slashed to death with a sword. Some of these people with faith were so destitute, persecuted, and mistreated that they were forced to hide in mountains, caves, and holes in the ground (Hebrews 11:35-38).

Among the people who received the Hebrews letter were those who had suffered, been insulted, and persecuted. Yet they accepted the confiscation of their property joyfully; they stood their ground in the face of suffering. They lived out their faith (Hebrews 10:32-34).

It's pretty clear, then, that faith is not a first-class ticket to a breezy life. When things aren't going so great—or even when they are—it helps to check out the examples of others who, through faith, stayed close to God—particularly, the Ultimate Example: the Father's Son.

"Therefore, since we are surrounded by such a great cloud of witnesses, let us throw off everything that hinders and the sin that so easily entangles, and let us run with perseverance the race marked out for us. Let us fix our eyes on Jesus, the Author and Perfecter of our faith, who for the joy set before Him endured the cross, scorning its shame, and sat down at the right hand of the throne of God" (Hebrews 12:1-2).

The lives of people who have lived by faith, the Hebrews-11-type people and others, surround us like a great cumulus cloud. These lives testify about faith. They shout to us, eloquently, "Faith is the only way to make sense out of frustrations, disappointments, and pain."

Or to pick up the athletic analogy: We are running around in the arena of life on this planet. We are surrounded by faithful people in the stands who understand the race because they too have run in it. They lived their lives consistently, true to God, so that their style of life has become one thunderous cheer: F-A-I-T-H!

Problem: Faith has obstacles. "Throw off everything that hinders and the sin that so easily entangles." Sin is not compatible with faith, that's clear. Sin trips us up. Living by faith while playing with sin is like trying to run a race in a suit of armor. But overt sin is not the only obstacle. Even seemingly good things can get in the way and hold us back from our best. These hindrances are the things that come between us and Jesus—maybe a relationship that means more to us than God does; or something we like to do, or a place we like to go.

As for the Ultimate Example, Jesus: He's the Completer of our faith—Author and Perfecter. He showed us how it works, even when we're pushed to the limit of adversity. Even as the Romans pounded spikes through His body, nailing Him to rugged, hand-hewn planks, He still trusted His Father.

"Faith is being sure of what we hope for and certain of what we do not see" (Hebrews 11:1). The Father's Son has completed the cycle. He's in heaven and has obtained the title to what His death and resurrection were to accomplish. He has completed faith. Someday it will all be out in the open when the Son returns and His followers join Him.

"Consider Him who endured such opposition from sinful men, so that you will not grow weary and lose heart" (Hebrews 12:3).

Cost-Counting and the Father Figure

A guy named Asaph once wrote a song and dedicated it to God. In the song, he spelled out his large frustrations. He looked around and noted that it was the wicked people who seemed to find the good life. "As for me," he complained, "my feet had almost slipped" (Psalm 73:2).

Asaph was honest enough to say what a lot of us only think: *Why doesn't God give His people special treatment? And, if not that, why not at least a fair shake? If anything, the bad guys seem to get the goods.*

In this, Christianity is straightforward and painfully honest. Until the Second Invasion of the Son, Christianity will be the minority opinion. Therefore, anyone who decides to sign up as a follower of the Son might just as well count the cost at the outset (Luke 14:25-35).

Remember, "In your struggle against sin, you have not yet resisted to the point of shedding your blood" (Hebrews 12:4).

Aside from whatever this suggests about determination, it also reminds us that for some, there will be the extreme cost—their own lives. At the time these Jewish Christians received the Hebrews letter, they had suffered persecution, but apparently not this most costly type: martyrdom. But it had already happened in Jerusalem. Stephen had been stoned (Acts 7:60); James had been stabbed (12:2).

But what purpose could God possibly have in permitting all this adversity?

"You have forgotten the word of encouragement that addresses you as sons: 'My son, do not make light of the Lord's discipline, and do not lose heart when He rebukes you, because the Lord disciplines those He loves, and He punishes everyone He accepts as a son' " (Hebrews 12:5-6).

This much is obvious: Hardship goes along with sonship. It was *normal* for all those Hebrews-11-people to have hassles. And it was normal for Jesus to go through great conflict and suffering. So, as might be expected, it is normal for us to experience frustration, disappointment, pain.

Sometimes God uses suffering as an instrument of discipline. If we've persisted in rebelliousness, He may get our attention through hardship. Paul spells it out: "Many among you are weak and sick, and a number of you have fallen asleep [died]. But if we judged ourselves, we would not come under judgment. When we are judged by the Lord, we are being disciplined so that we will not be condemned with the world" (1 Corinthians 11:30-32). The

Apostle John also suggested that sin sometimes leads to death (1 John 5:16-17).

And yet, suffering is not always a result of sin. A person doesn't get the mumps because of his iniquity. Often—probably, most often—our suffering and hardship come as the natural result of living in an abnormal world—a world at odds with God.

As Jesus walked down the dusty Palestinian roads with His disciples one day, they came across a man blind from birth. The disciples wanted to know if that man's sins caused him to be born blind, or if his parents did the sinning and thereby caused the problem. "Neither," Jesus informed them. "This happened so that the work of God might be displayed in his life" (John 9:1-3). For sure, that is often the case. We just don't always get to see God do His work.

But there is something else related to the why behind our hassles. "You may have had to suffer grief in all kinds of trials. These have come so that your faith—of greater worth than gold, which perishes even though refined by fire—may be proved genuine and may result in praise, glory, and honor when Jesus Christ is revealed" (1 Peter 1:6-7).

Jesus has an investment in our life development. Our struggles increase the value of His investment; as we respond in faith, they make us better people. There's a design behind God's discipline.

The Crane at the Arcade

You see all kinds at a carnival. But the thing that caught my eye was a sandy-haired kid with a generous sprinkling of freckles. He was oblivious to the swirl of activity around him. His eyes were riveted to a box about the size of a phone booth, except shorter. Inside its glass panels was a huge pile of the nicest looking junk you could imagine—and a few fine items as well. There, in the middle of that glass-boxed pile of goodies, was a crane. The object was clear: feed the coin-guzzling machine for the privilege of using the crane to fish for prizes.

I watched this kid for a while and noticed that he was genuinely determined. It was obvious from the pocket full of change he poured into the coin slot and the look of intense concentration on his face.

I thought of that scene recently, as I watched skilled construction workers raising a multilevel building. In both cases—the kid and the construction crew—the crane became an extension of the person to accomplish a purpose. A highly skilled operator can do some remarkable things with the equipment.

It occurs to me that we're urged in Hebrews 12 to see hardship as a tool God is using, a piece of awkward, heavy equipment He is utilizing in our construction. We look at the suffering that comes our way and it appears cold as steel, impersonal, ominous—even deadly at times. But beyond the machinery that may at times appear to be out of control, the wise and loving Father is accomplishing His incomprehensible purpose.

"Endure hardship as discipline; God is treating you as sons. For what son is not disciplined by his father? If you are not disciplined (and everyone undergoes discipline), then you are illegitimate children and not true sons.

"Moreover, we have all had human fathers who disciplined us and we respected them for it. How much more should we submit to the Father of our spirits and live! Our fathers disciplined us for a little while as they thought best; but God disciplines us for our good, that we may share in His holiness. No discipline seems pleasant at the time, but painful. Later on however, it produces a harvest of righteousness and peace for those who have been trained by it" (Hebrews 12:7-11).

As much as we chafe under it, most of us are wise enough to see the value in the parental discipline we have had to endure. It's just part of the family process. When we get a bit older and start exerting our independence, the discipline concept gets muddled. But it's still there.

The point is, through the process of maturity we should learn to appreciate our parents' discipline. If we can understand that, we should for sure grasp the importance of a right response to the discipline that comes from God, the Father of our spirit.

I often think, *God sure has sassy kids.* He urges us toward holiness. We run off, independent of Him, trying to assert our independence. In other words, it seems that the family of God is constantly going through adolescent-type hassles. In an earthly family, a certain amount of that tension and conflict is to be expected; teens are moving toward adulthood. But in the family of God, there is a sense in which we are to continue to have a childlike dependence—faith. Asserting ourselves in rebellion is always inappropriate in our relationship with God, even though we *are* to become full-grown, mature Christians (Ephesians 4:14-15).

But, just as Hebrews 12 presents the childlike side of our Christianity, so it presents the mature, adult-like side. In doing so, the writer returns to the athlete image:

"Therefore, strengthen your feeble arms and weak knees! 'Make level paths for your feet,' so that the lame may not be disabled, but rather healed" (Hebrews 12:12-13).

A person with feeble arms and weak knees is ready to collapse. In our relationship with God, the condition can come on us almost without our knowing it. "If you think you are standing firm," Paul cautioned, "be careful that you don't fall!" (1 Corinthians 10:12)

As for the reference to the lame: A person who can't quite walk right doesn't go rock-climbing and may not be thrilled with stairs. Instead, if he can find a nice, level walkway he may be able to get by without compounding his injury. An immature Christian, lacking discernment, often tries to run around on the rocky ground of rebellion. It's kind of like the hindrances and entangling sins the writer to the Hebrews (12:1) warns us of.

Flying Solo with Clipped Wings

I think again of David and how crushed he felt over his frustrated career plans and his difficult family relationships. The pain he felt was greatly intensified because he had no one to share the hassles with—no one to help him find warmth from the Father of the Son.

God often uses tangled experiences to nudge us toward Himself. Somehow it's easier to get the message when we have close and supportive relationships with other Christians. We were never intended to fly solo, as angelic as we may feel—a point made clear in Hebrews. In our hardships, we are to remain teachable, not become bitter. At the same time, we are never to forget our brothers and sisters in the family of God.

"Make every effort to live in peace with all men and to be holy; without holiness no one will see the Lord. See to it that no one misses the grace of God and that no bitter root grows up to cause trouble and defile many. See that no one is sexually immoral, or is godless like Esau, who for a single meal sold his inheritance rights as the oldest son. Afterward, as you know, when he wanted to inherit this blessing, he was rejected. He could bring about no change of mind, though he sought the blessing with tears" (Hebrews 12:14-17).

The bitter root is unbelief—lack of faith. And that makes a forceful point. Faith is not optional equipment for Followers of the Son. "Without faith it is impossible to please God" (Hebrews 11:6).

When a person lacks faith, he can rarely handle frustration, disappointment, and pain without becoming bitter and cynical. Life on the Son's Planet tosses too many confusing questions our way. We cannot handle them without a seed of trust, planted in God.

But the writer wants us to understand too that a bitter root of unbelief in one person begins to affect other people as well. Doubt and anxiety are contagious, like whooping cough. Just as we cannot make faith a solo flight, so we rarely crash alone; almost always we take others with us. We pull them away from God—if only slightly.

There is warmth from the Father of the Son—for ourselves and for the entire family of God. But if we refuse to come in faith, that warmth soon becomes blistering heat.

As Prodigal sat in the center of the highway, he'd been so taken with the novelty of his light-emitting Book that he'd not noticed the shadows retreating from a breathtaking scarlet Sonrise. But the warmth came rapidly—more rapidly than he expected. Soon the heat was pounding on him as it had before his encounter with the Son—only hotter.

For the first time since running into the Son, he felt he was the object of the Son's penetrating rays rather than a participant in them. The heat seemed violent, not friendly.

Once again he found himself fearful. Only hours earlier it was the deepening darkness that had terrified him. Now he felt sure this Sonshine he thought he understood would consume him in a great pulsating fireball.

Instinctively, Prodigal stood. Immediately the temperature seemed to fall. Then, almost on impulse, he again began walking westward, *toward* that great Source of heat and light. As he did so, rather than the heat increasing, gradually it subsided until it equalized at an even, comfortable level. Gradually Prodigal became conscious of warmth but not heat.

And his mind returned to the Book:

"A follower of the Son cannot settle in the darkness as if at home, for his ultimate home is the blazing core of the Son itself."

12

Why does one person turn to God and remain
true, while another resists and turns away?
Perhaps there is no clear-cut answer. But this
much is certain: There has to be
a changed life . . .

After the
Cosmic Encounter

It was one of those friendships that is "close" from
a distance. Since we were separated by a couple
thousand miles, we only saw each other every two
or three years. And a lot of things can change in
that much time.

Glenn was a couple years older than I and was
often left to himself by family and friends. I suppose that's why I had such a concern for him. I was
always afraid that he would get in serious trouble—
not just for some prank or practical joke, either. He
was sullen and had a violent temper. And it wasn't
as if he had a good example to pattern his life after.
I'm not sure what kept his parents together, but it
wasn't mutual love or tenderness.

I was surprised when Glenn showed up in
California with his new bride, Sherri. It was the
first time I had seen Glenn happy, calm, outgoing.
Perhaps being so far from home had caused Glenn

and Sherri to rely on each other more; I don't know. But Glenn had an almost boyish love and tenderness for Sherri.

Eventually, this separation from family and friends wore them down, and Glenn and Sherri became lonely until they were no longer capable of handling their feelings. Besides, California wasn't all Glenn had convinced himself it would be, nor did he now consider his family as distasteful as he had before. So he quit his job and the couple returned "home."

Two or three years later, things again changed for Glenn. He developed a strong alcohol and drug dependence and his violent temper reasserted itself. He dumped Sherri, leaving her to care for their newborn. From then on things rapidly deteriorated, until within a few years even his health was broken.

As I reflect on Glenn's life, I see a person who started out in some ways disadvantaged. He came close to a significant change in his lifestyle, but he turned away from his opportunity. After that, his life was a rapid downward spiral.

In contrast to Glenn, I think of Scott who, while still in high school, resolved that his life would be different—different from the commonplace. Scott had heard people share their "testimonies" of how they had wandered far from God, compromised their moral convictions, later regretted it, and had returned to Christianity.

He kept thinking of all the time they'd wasted and all they'd missed out on.

Even as a junior high school student, Scott had been aware of the spiritual search of his friends and had organized a Bible club at his school. Attendance grew from 30 to 900. Throughout his teen years, he built on that early experience and God used him in unexpected ways.

And why shouldn't we take Christianity seriously! Even in our youth.

Deb started out that way too. She demonstrated even in her early teens that Jesus, God's One Final Blazing Word, was her big priority.

Deb seemed to have the ability to withstand peer-group pressure without alienating the people around her. "You don't have to eat garbage," she chided her friends, "to know what it tastes like." Everyone respected her for those strong, solid convictions.

But the convictions began to crumble in her late teens, and collapsed altogether in her early 20s. Deb now faces an awesome accountability. She turned her back on the Son.

The writer to the Hebrews warns: There must be a changed life after the Cosmic Encounter. Things can never again be the same.

More than a Magic Kingdom

The Hebrews letter was written to Christian Jews who were considering dropping the Christianity. Since they were facing persecution for following the Son, it seemed smart to drop the commitment. In their thinking, if they dropped the Son they could merely pick up where they left off in their Jewish religion. The Hebrews letter declared pointedly, that without the Son-Word, even Old Testament Jewish religion was now meaningless. Jesus was God's One Final Blazing Word, sent to complete that old system. He was given as the substance toward which all the old shadows had pointed—old shadows such as the giving of the Law on Mt. Sinai.

"You have not come to a mountain that can be touched and that is burning with fire; to darkness, gloom, and storm, to a trumpet blast or to such a voice speaking words, so that those who heard it begged that no further word be spoken to them, because they could not bear what was commanded: 'If even an animal touches the mountain, it must be stoned.' The sight was so terrifying that Moses said, 'I am trembling with fear' " (Hebrews 12:18-21).

The point: It was a scary day when God gave Moses the Law. (Exodus 19—20 and Deuteronomy 4 paint a vivid picture.) When God spoke with Moses, He gave *commandments*, not polite requests. Since the writer to the Hebrews presents Jesus Christ as far greater than the Old Testament Law, how much more important is it to follow Him?

"You have come to Mount Zion, to the heavenly Jerusalem, the city of the living God. You have come to thousands upon thousands of angels in joyful assembly, to the church of the firstborn, whose names are written in heaven. You have come to God, the Judge of all men, to the spirits of righteous men made perfect, to Jesus the Mediator of a new covenant, and to the sprinkled blood that speaks a better word than the blood of Abel" (Hebrews 12:22-24).

Abraham had looked forward "to the city with foundations, whose Architect and Builder is God" (11:10). Under the Son-Word System, it is as if we have actually entered that city. It is alive with celebration of the Son Himself—the kind of celebration that comes with attaining something you have hoped for, of finally seeing what has for so long been unseen. This is a city inhabited by people who have at last been made righteous because of the Son's blood.

Once a person has been exposed to all of this, how can he turn away and hike back into the darkness?

We have to accept it: There has to be a Friendly Invasion of the Son-Word. Once there is, we can never again be the same.

"See to it that you do not refuse Him who speaks. If they did not escape when they refused Him who warned them on earth, how much less will we, if we turn away from Him who warns us from heaven? At that time His voice shook the earth, but now He has promised, 'Once more I will shake not only the earth but also the heavens.' The words 'once more' indicate the removing of what can be shaken—that is, created things—so that what cannot be shaken may remain" (Hebrews 12:25-27).

When God thundered His commandments on Mt. Sinai, the earth literally shook (Exodus 19:11-20). He has now given warning from heaven. A future day is coming when He will shake all of creation to its foundations. At that time, the only things that will endure are those linked to Him.

It's another way of saying that we can receive the *Friendly* Invasion of the Son-Word *now*. But if we do not accept His Friendly Invasion, we must face Him in judgment when He invades in fury to crush the mutiny on the Son's Planet.

"Therefore, since we are receiving a kingdom that cannot be shaken, let us be thankful, and so worship God acceptably with reverence and awe, for our God is a consuming fire" (Hebrews 12:28-29).

After Invasion One

I think of such pointed warnings as that and I wonder. I wonder about Glenn who, to my knowledge, never accepted the Son's Friendly Invasion. His life and his forever-existence can be shaken until they buckle, then crumble. I am really scared for Glenn. I visualize his life falling in around him, pulverizing him in judgment, the Sonshine of God scorching his eternity.

I wonder about Deb. I know she walked an aisle one time or other, prayed a prayer; I know she said, "Jesus, come into my life." I guess she was counseled, "OK, Deb, since you've asked Jesus into your life, where is He now?" I can almost hear her responding simply, "In my heart." But I wonder. Does she know that her own "heart" can deceive her? (Jeremiah 17:9) Does she know that words alone are not enough? (Matthew 7:21-23) Does she know that a changed life follows faith? (2 Corinthians 5:17)

I wonder about Scott. I wonder what joyful celebration will welcome him into Son City. I wonder what it will be like for him to meet dozens of people who are citizens of that city because he took the time to introduce them. And I wonder just how glad Scott will be that his life was changed by the Cosmic Encounter.

Brothers, Strangers, Prisoners, Angels

I suppose with persecution all around, it would be tempting to develop social amnesia. A friend is harrassed or arrested for his faith. Suddenly you forget you know him. Peter did that with Jesus—denied

Him repeatedly the night of His arrest (Matthew 26:69-75).

But a changed life means *hospitality*—even when it's difficult.

"Keep on loving each other as brothers. Do not forget to entertain strangers, for by so doing some people have entertained angels without knowing it. Remember those in prison as if you were their fellow prisoners, and those who are mistreated as if you yourselves were suffering" (Hebrews 13:1-3).

Love is the principle (13:1). This love must be self-sacrificing. Jesus identified this as an un- mistakable badge of a life that's been changed (John 13:34-35).

The principle gets specific. If we love, *we will not turn away strangers* (13:2). This is a central theme of an often-neglected, one-chapter New Testament letter, 3 John. But the theme is repeated throughout the Bible. Believers were urged to open their homes to traveling Christians as an ex- pression of love and hospitality. After all, they couldn't check into a Holiday Inn or Best Western and charge it to the church. As for entertaining angels: Since they didn't flutter in on silken wings, one could never hype up special treatment for such divine company. Even so, the angels came, carrying out their special assignments for God (a few exam- ples: Genesis 18:1-3; 19:1-2; Judges 6:11-24; 13:6-20).

Love reaches between the bars (Hebrews 13:3). God has already praised these people on this ac- count. "You sympathized with those in prison" (10:34). Now they are urged to keep it up. The Book of Philippians is a thank-you letter to the church for living out the instructions given them in Hebrews 13:3.

Of Love and Money

A changed life means *purity*—even when it's the minority opinion.

"Marriage should be honored by all, and the marriage bed kept pure, for God will judge the adulterer and all the sexually immoral" (Hebrews 13:4).

It's a fun reminder: God regards marriage and the sex that is so much a part of it as good, and more than good—*pure*. God wants it kept that way. God identifies two things that crud up the purity of marriage-sex. *Adultery* dirties it. You can't have intimate encounters with people other than your marriage partner-for-life without corrupting God's good gift.

"All the sexually immoral" includes all other sex sins, especially sex before marriage. Contrary to common opinion, sexual encounters before marriage tarnish God's real thing. It's not that God is anti-fun; it's that He is pro-purity. He designed pleasure to flourish in an atmosphere of purity.

To have a changed life after the Cosmic Encounter, means then that we have an observable *hospitality* and an observable *purity*. A changed life also means *serenity*—even when life is confusing.

"Keep your lives free from the love of money and be content with what you have, because God has said, 'Never will I leave you; never will I forsake you.' So we say with confidence, 'The Lord is my Helper; I will not be afraid. What can man do to me?' " (Hebrews 13:5-6)

What can man do to me? He can repossess my wall-to-wall stereo, bought on time at an outrageous interest rate.

What can man do to me? He can fail to solve world problems and bring severe financial reversals. Our nation could become as poor and needy as any so-called underdeveloped nation. There might be famine; a new car would then be of marginal value.

What can man do to me? Plenty. And nothing.

The Friendly Invasion of the Son-Word means my values can change. The things I have regarded as essential fade in their importance. The Son teaches me to be content—not just in prosperity, but also in poverty.

Jesus challenges us to put worry aside, accepting the reality of a loving Father (Matthew 6:25-34). Paul says contentment is a lesson that can be learned regardless of circumstances (Philippians 4:10-13).

Our values are the bottom line: "Keep your lives free from the love of money and be content with what you have" (Hebrews 13:5). It may seem too obvious to say, but loving money is tied to loving the things money provides. It seems easy to say, "Oh, I don't love money." It's not so easy to say, "I do not love *things.*"

Remember the Leaders: the Good and the Bad

After the Cosmic Encounter, when we begin new life in the Son, we depend on one another for growth. I think of a friend who had made a vague, though possibly genuine commitment to the Son but had then wandered. Everyone was ecstatic when he returned to Christianity. Soon after his return, he attached himself, like a barnacle, to a nice girl. But, nice or not, she was involved in a non-Christian religious group. He didn't have the spiritual insight to see the difference. "Religion is religion, isn't it?" he questioned.

"Remember your leaders, who spoke the Word of God to you. Consider the outcome of their way of life and imitate their faith. Jesus Christ is the same yesterday and today and forever" (Hebrews 13:7-8).

"Who spoke the Word of God"—correct teaching. Preachers like to call it "doctrine." If the religious leader has wrong doctrine, don't follow him. And how can you know? Personal Bible study.

"Their way of life . . . their faith"—correct lifestyle. If the style of life does not match Bible teaching, don't copy it. Jesus has not changed His mind on doctrine, nor has He altered the manual when it comes to lifestyle. Know the Bible. Follow it.

"Do not be carried away by all kinds of strange teachings. It is good for our hearts to be strengthened by grace, not by ceremonial foods, which are of no value to those who eat them. We have an altar from which those who minister at the tabernacle have no right to eat" (Hebrews 13:9-10).

There have always been religious leaders who try to take the Son-Word System (faith in Jesus) and twist it into a system of do's and don'ts. Their idea is that if we are nice enough, God's gate swings open on its hinges. Contrary to that, the righteous live by faith (Hebrews 10:38-11:40).

"The high priest carries the blood of animals into the Most Holy Place as a sin offering, but the bodies are burned outside the camp. And so Jesus also suffered outside the city gate to make the people holy through His own blood. Let us, then, go to Him outside the camp, bearing the disgrace He bore. For here we do not have an enduring city, but we are looking for the city that is to come" (Hebrews 13:11-14).

True, Christianity is a minority opinion. But faith is not based on the latest poll. "Faith is being sure of what we hope for and certain of what we do not see" (11:1). For us, that faith has to be tied to the City of the Son, the future which is in the hands of God's One Final Blazing Word. "We fix our eyes not on what is seen," Paul stressed, "but on what is unseen. For what is seen is temporary, but what is unseen is eternal" (2 Corinthians 4:18).

"Through Jesus, therefore, let us continually offer to God a sacrifice of praise—the fruit of lips that confess His name. And do not forget to do good and to share with others, for with such sacrifices God is pleased.

"Obey your leaders and submit to their authority. They keep watch over you as men who must give an account. Obey them so that their work will be a joy, not a burden, for that would be of no advantage to you" (Hebrews 13:15-17).

This Late Word Just In . . .

Prayer is a big priority. The Friendly Invasion of the Son-Word is the *beginning* of a new relationship. It is one element in keeping close to the Son after the Cosmic Encounter.

"Pray for us. We are sure that we have a clear conscience and desire to live honorably in every way. I particularly urge you to pray so that I may be restored to you soon.

"May the God of peace, who through the blood

of the eternal covenant brought back from the
dead our Lord Jesus, that great Shepherd of the
sheep, equip you with everything good for doing
His will, and may He work in us what is pleasing to
Him, through Jesus Christ, to whom be glory forever and ever. Amen" (Hebrews 13:18-21).

For sure, living in Sonshine does not happen because of our own brilliance. I think again of Scott.
God was able to use him because his life changed
after the Cosmic Encounter. But Scott will not get a
great galactic pat on the back. The credit goes to
the Son Himself.

My thoughts return to my friend Glenn, who
obstinately refused the warmth of the Son's love,
and to Deb who turned her back on it. It haunts me.
To turn away the Friendly Invasion of the Son-
Word is to invite the hellish reality of judgment.

But as I read Hebrews, I pick up the vibration
that someone cared deeply about his readers. He
had watched them as they seemed to find New
Life, as they sizzled in joy from their Cosmic Encounter with the Son. The author had witnessed
too how they had been bombarded by frustration,
disappointment, and pain. He had watched as some
wandered off into the darkness, leaving the Son behind them. He wrote to say, "Only God's One Final
Blazing Word can give hope in your frazzled experiences."

Things haven't changed all that much over the
years. We too face frustration, disappointment, and
pain. And still there are those who insist: "The only
enduring hope that can be salvaged from our
tangled experiences comes as we keep on living in
Sonshine."

Walking close to the Sonshine, Prodigal discovered that though he encountered oppressive darkness or enjoyed spectacular radiance, he was always given insight into his situations. This insight was itself startling.

Prodigal had assumed he journeyed on a deserted highway. With his new insight he saw that it was actually a congested thoroughfare on which most everyone traveled east. Only occasionally did he see another west-bound pilgrim.

He soon learned the importance of speaking encouragements to other west-bound followers of the Son. Even when he was unable to get near them due to the press of the crowd, he would shout to them, knowing he'd be heard above the noise.

He began to notice opportunities he never knew existed to point the east-bound to the Son.

Significantly, Prodigal learned the importance of continual movement toward the Son. It had been revealed in the Book, that the Sonshine would one day invade the darkness in fury, dispelling it. This Book referred to as the Son's Great Day. At the time, each person's progress either toward or away from the Son would be forever fixed.

Most encouragingly, Prodigal discovered that he was known to the Son by a new name. It was not a name suggesting waywardness and rebellion, but a name of honor and position that would be revealed on that Great Day of the Son.